Presented to

....

By

....

On the occasion of

....

Date

....

Fifty

GOLDEN YEARS

A PHOTOGRAPHIC CELEBRATION
OF THE
REIGN OF HM QUEEN ELIZABETH II

EAGLE, GUILDFORD

A STEADY INFLUENCE
IN A CHANGING WORLD

The world has changed greatly in the past 50 years. When Her Majesty Queen Elizabeth II came to the throne in 1952, space travel was still a dream and computers were just mechanical calculators. TV was in its infancy and it was the 1953 Coronation itself that launched TV as a popular communication and entertainment medium.

But all through that half century of change, some things have remained constant. The monarchy, although itself much changed in its public image, is one of the key structures that give British life its distinctive shape and stability.

The great state occasions – from occasional royal weddings to the annual opening of Parliament – give us all an opportunity to witness the colourful ceremonial that evokes the eternal values of human life undergirding the desires and needs of the daily grind.

Even the Queen's formal role in approving Acts of Parliament and appointments of bishops reminds us that there is an authority higher than elected governments and wise advisers, and to which all are answerable.

Indeed, the Queen has herself acknowledged (in her 2000 Christmas address) "The teachings of Christ and my own personal accountability before God provide a framework in which I try to lead my life." And therein lies the key to the monarchy's endurance.

For it is more than an institution, important as that is. The monarchy is embodied by a person. The Queen's own dedication to duty is legendary, dating from her amazingly mature speech to the nation before she was Queen, at the age of 21: "My whole life, whether it be long or short, shall be devoted to your service and the service of the great imperial family to which we all belong."

With her genuine sympathy for people who suffer, and sustained by her quiet but definite Christian faith, she has preserved that framework of stability and order so necessary to a nation.

So this book is more than just a memento of the past 50 years, although you will certainly find within it a year-by-year summary of the international, sporting and arts events which have taken place. You will also read key messages given by the Queen in that year, revealing in her own words the faith and values that have sustained and motivated her.

Taken together they provide a fitting tribute to a remarkable person who has kept faith with her country, her people, her principles and her God. Without her quiet influence (often in the background, as biographies of several Prime Ministers testify), and her steady public presence, this nation would be much poorer in a spiritual and constitutional sense.

Thank you, Ma'am, for your example of service, tolerance and integrity.

God save the Queen!

The Publishers

Each Christmas, at this time, my beloved father broadcast a message to his people in all parts of the world. Today I am doing this to you, who are now my people. As he used to do, I am speaking to you from my own home, where I am spending Christmas with my family: and let me say at once how I hope that your children are enjoying themselves as much as mine are on a day which is especially the children's festival, kept in honour of the Child born at Bethlehem nearly 2000 years ago.

Most of you to whom I am speaking will be in your own homes, but I have a special thought for those who are serving their country in distant lands far from their families. Wherever you are, either at home or away, in snow or in sunshine, I give you my affectionate greetings, with every good wish for Christmas and the New Year.

At Christmas our thoughts are always full of our homes and our families. This is the day when members of the same family try to come together, or if separated by distance or event meet in spirit and affection by exchanging greetings.

But we belong, you and I, to a far larger family. We belong, all of us, to the British Commonwealth and Empire, that immense union of nations, with their homes set in all the four corners of the earth. Like our own families, it can be a great power for good – a force which I believe can be of immeasurable benefit to all humanity. My father and my grandfather before him worked all their lives to unite our peoples ever more closely, and to maintain its ideals which were so near to their hearts. I shall strive to carry on their work.

Already you have given me strength to do so, for, since my accession 10 months ago, your loyalty and affection have been an immense support and encouragement. I want to take this Christmas Day, my first opportunity, to thank you with all my heart.

Many grave problems and difficulties confront us all, but with a new faith in the old and splendid beliefs given us by our forefathers, and the strength to venture beyond the safeties of the past, I know we shall be worthy of our duty.

Above all, we must keep alive that courageous spirit of adventure that is the finest quality of youth: and by youth I do not just mean those who are young in years; I mean, too, all those who are young in heart, no matter how old they may be. That spirit still flourishes in this old country and in all the younger countries of our Commonwealth.

On this broad foundation let us set out to build a truer knowledge of ourselves and our fellow men, to work for tolerance and understanding among the nations, and to use the tremendous forces of science and learning for the betterment of man's lot upon this earth. If we can do these three things with courage, with generosity and with humility, then surely we shall achieve that "peace on earth, good will toward men" which is the eternal message of Christmas, and the desire of us all.

At my Coronation next June I shall dedicate myself anew to your service. I shall do so in the presence of a great congregation, drawn from every part of the Commonwealth and Empire, while millions outside Westminster Abbey will hear the promises and the prayers being offered up within its walls, and see much of the ancient ceremony in which kings and queens before me have taken part through century upon century.

You will be keeping it as a holiday: but I want to ask you all, whatever your religion may be, to pray for me on that day – to pray that God may give me wisdom and strength to carry out the solemn promises I shall be making, and that I may faithfully serve him, and you, all the days of my life.

May God bless and guide you all through the coming year.

Right:
Queen Elizabeth II and Prince Philip, Duke of Edinburgh, with their children, Prince Charles and Princess Anne, entertaining their guests, King Faisal II of Iraq and the Regent of Iraq (left) in the grounds of Balmoral Castle, Scotland.

1952

World Events of 1952

Eisenhower is elected President of the United States.

16,000 people escape from East to West Berlin in one month.

America explodes the hydrogen bomb.

King George VI dies.

The diary of Anne Frank is published.

In Cyprus, Greeks attack British forces and Turkish minority.

Britain develops its first atomic bomb.

Crown Prince Hussein becomes King of Jordan at the age of 17.

The Nobel Peace Prize is awarded to Albert Schweitzer.

President Truman officially ends the war in the Pacific.

The world's first atomic-powered submarine is launched in the US.

The US liner 'United States' crosses the Atlantic in a record three days, ten hours and 40 minutes.

Eva Peron, the Argentinian politician, dies.

Sporting Life

The Olympic Games are held in Helsinki.

17-year-old Maureen 'Little Mo' Connolly wins Wimbledon.

The Australian tennis team wins the Davis Cup.

In cricket, Australia defeats the West Indies 4 Tests to 1.

The United States win 43 gold medals at the Olympic Games.

The Arts

'East of Eden' by John Steinbeck is published.

It is the world premiere of Charlie Chaplin's film 'Limelight'.

Samuel Beckett publishes 'Waiting for Godot'.

Left:
Maria Callas, pictured here with Tito Gobi and Renato Cioni, stunned the audience at Covent Garden when she made her debut singing the title role in Bellini's 'Norma'.

Opera singer Maria Callas is "discovered" at the Royal Opera House, Covent Garden.

Agatha Christie's latest play 'The Mousetrap' opens in London.

Hit songs are 'I'm Singing in the Rain' and 'It Takes Two to Tango'.

Ernest Hemingway's novel 'The Old Man and the Sea' is published.

1953

World Events of 1953

Sir Winston Churchill wins the Nobel Prize for literature.

Joseph Stalin dies.

A vaccine against polio is successfully tested.

Everest is conquered by Edmund Hillary and Sherpa Tensing.

The Korean War ends.

Britain recognises the Republic of Egypt.

The coronation of Queen Elizabeth II is held.

Stiletto heels are the latest fashion in footwear.

John F. Kennedy marries Jacqueline Bouvier.

The new Ford Popular is launched; at £390 it is the cheapest car on the British market.

Eisenhower is inaugurated as President of the US.

A record 30,031 new houses are built in one month in the UK.

The US Supreme Court considers banning racial segregation in schools.

Sporting Life

In England, football star Stanley Matthews helps Blackpool win their first ever FA Cup final.

In tennis, 18-year-old Ken Rosewall wins the Australian Singles Title.

Jim Peters is the first man to run a marathon in under 2 hours 20 minutes.

English cricketers regain the Ashes from the Australians after 20 years.

American tennis player Maureen Connolly wins the Grand Slam.

In football, Arsenal win the League Championship for a record seventh time.

The Arts

In Paris, Samuel Beckett's play 'Waiting for Godot' is premiered.

Ernest Hemingway wins a Pulitzer Prize for 'The Old Man and the Sea' and 'Picnic'.

Hit songs are 'Diamonds are a Girl's Best Friend', 'How Much is that Doggy in the Window?' and 'I Love Paris'.

Left and below: Queen Elizabeth II was crowned in Westminster Abbey on June 2nd 1953. The procession and entire ceremony were broadcast live on television.

Far left: Thousands lined the procession route and those who wanted a good place camped overnight in the rain.

Last Christmas I spoke to you from England. This year I am doing so from New Zealand. Auckland, which I reached only two days ago, is, I suppose, as far as any city in the world from London, and I have travelled some thousands of miles through many changing scenes and climates on my voyage here.

Despite all that, however, I find myself today completely and most happily at home. Of course, we all want our children at Christmas time, for that is the season above all others when each family gathers at its own hearth. I hope that perhaps mine are listening to me now, and I am sure that when the time comes they too will be great travellers.

My husband and I left London a month ago, but we have already paid short visits to Bermuda, Jamaica, Fiji and Tonga, and have passed through Panama. I should like to thank all our hosts very warmly for the kindness of their welcome and the great pleasure of our stay.

In a short time we shall be visiting Australia and, later, Ceylon, and before we end this great journey we shall catch a glimpse of other places in Asia, Africa and in the Mediterranean.

So this will be a voyage right round the world – the first that a Queen of England has been privileged to make as Queen.

But what is really important to me is that I set out on this journey in order to see as much as possible of the people and countries of the Commonwealth and Empire, to learn at first hand something of their triumphs and difficulties and something of their hopes and fears.

At the same time, I want to show that the Crown is not merely an abstract symbol of our unity but a personal and living bond between you and me.

Some people have expressed the hope that my reign may mark a new Elizabethan age. Frankly, I do not myself feel at all like my great Tudor forebear, who was blessed with neither husband nor children, who ruled as a despot and was never able to leave her native shores.

But there is at least one very significant resemblance between her age and mine. For her Kingdom, small though it may have been and poor by comparison with her European neighbours, was yet great in spirit and well endowed with men who were ready to encompass the earth.

Now, this great Commonwealth, of which I am so proud to be the head, and of which that ancient Kingdom forms a part, though rich in material resources is richer still in the enterprise and courage of its peoples.

Little did those adventurous heroes of Tudor and Stuart times realise what would grow from the settlements which there pioneers founded.

From the Empire of which they built the frame there has arisen a world-wide fellowship of nations of a type never seen before.

In that fellowship, the United Kingdom, is an equal partner with many other proud and independent nations, and she is leading yet other still backward nations forward to the same goal.

All the nations have helped to create our Commonwealth, and all are equally concerned to maintain, develop and defend it against any challenge that may come.

As I travel across the world today, I am ever more deeply impressed with the achievement and the opportunity which the modern Commonwealth presents.

Like New Zealand, from whose North Island I am speaking, every one of its nations can be justly proud of what it has built for itself on its own soil. But their greatest achievement, I suggest, is the Commonwealth itself, and that owes much to all of them.

Thus formed, the Commonwealth bears no resemblance to the empires of the past. It is an entirely new conception – built on the highest qualities of the spirit of man: friendship, loyalty and the desire for freedom and peace.

To that new conception of an equal partnership of nations and races, I shall give myself heart and soul every day of my life.

I wished to speak of it from New Zealand this Christmas Day because we are celebrating the birth of the Prince of Peace, who preached the brotherhood of man. May that brotherhood be furthered by all our thoughts and deeds from year to year.

In pursuit of that supreme ideal the Commonwealth is moving steadily towards greater harmony between its many creeds, colours and races, despite the imperfections by which, like every human institution, it is beset.

Already, indeed, in the last half-century it has proved itself the most effective and progressive association of peoples which history has yet seen; and its ideal of brotherhood embraces the whole world.

To all my peoples throughout the Commonwealth I commend that Christmas hope and prayer.

And now I want to say something to my people in New Zealand. Last night a most grievous railway accident took place at Tangiwai which will have brought tragedy into many homes and sorrow into all on this Christmas Day.

I know that there is no one in New Zealand and, indeed, throughout the Commonwealth who will not join with my husband and me in sending to those who mourn a message of sympathy in their loss.

I pray that they and all who have been injured may be comforted and strengthened.

It is two years since my husband and I spent Christmas with our children. And as we do so to-day, we look back upon a Christmas spent last year in Auckland, in hot sunshine, 13,000 miles away.

Though this was strange for us, we felt at home there for we were among people who are my own people and whose affectionate greeting I shall remember all my life long. They surrounded us with kindness and friendship, as did all my people throughout the mighty sweep of our world-encircling journey.

Nevertheless, to all of us there is nothing quite like the family gathering in familiar surroundings, centred on the children whose festival this truly is, in the traditional atmosphere of love and happiness that springs from the enjoyment of simple, well-tried things.

When it is night and wind and rain beat upon the window the family is most conscious of the warmth and peacefulness that surround the pleasant fireside. So our Commonwealth hearth becomes more precious than ever before by the contrast between its homely security and the storm which sometimes seems to be brewing outside, in the darkness of uncertainty and doubt that envelops the whole world.

In the turbulence of this anxious and active world many people are leading uneventful lonely lives. To them dreariness, not disaster, is the enemy. They seldom realise that on their steadfastness, on their ability to withstand the fatigue of dull, repetitive work and on their courage in meeting constant small adversities, depend in great measure the happiness and prosperity of the community as a whole. When we look at the landscape of our life on this earth there is in the minds of all of us a tendency to admire the peaks, and to ignore the foothills and the fertile plain from which they spring. We praise – and rightly – the heroes whose resource and courage shine so brilliantly in moments of crisis.

We forget sometimes that behind the wearers of the Victoria or George Cross there stand ranks of unknown, unnamed men and women willing and able if the call came to render valiant service.

We are amazed by the spectacular discoveries in scientific knowledge, which should bring comfort and leisure to millions. We do not always reflect that these things also have rested to some extent on the faithful toil and devotion to duty of the great bulk of ordinary citizens.

The upward course of the nation's history is due in the long run to the soundness of heart of its average men and women.

And so it is that this Christmas Day I want to send a special message of encouragement and good cheer to those of you whose lot is cast in dull and unenvied surroundings, to those whose names will never be household words, but to whose work and loyalty we owe so much.

May you be proud to remember - as I am myself - how much depends on you and that even when your life seems most monotonous, what you do is always of real value and importance to your fellow-men.

I have referred to Christmas as the children's festival, but this lovely day is not only a time for family reunions, for paper decorations, for roast turkey and plum pudding.

It has, before all, its origin in the homage we pay to a very special family, who lived long ago in a very ordinary home, in a very unimportant village in the uplands of a small Roman province. Life in such a place might have been uneventful. But the light, kindled in Bethlehem and then streaming from the cottage window in Nazareth has illuminated the world for 2000 years.

It is in the glow of that bright beam that I wish you all a blessed Christmas and a happy New Year!

Top left:
Queen Elizabeth II, wearing her Coronation dress, arriving with the Duke of Edinburgh to open Parliment in Wellington, New Zealand.

Left:
Queen Elizabeth II, with Countess Edwina Mountbatten, Prince Charles (left) and Princess Anne arriving at the Marsa Ground in Malta to watch a Polo match.

1954

Right:
Jubilant crowds climb up to the Presidency's balcony to embrace Prime Minister Nasser.

Far right:
Roger Bannister broke the British record for the mile in 1953, and made his attempt to run the distance in under 4 minutes at Oxford in May 1954. His first record was broken by John Landy a few weeks later, but Bannister took the record again later that year at the Empire Games in Canada.

The Arts

The first Newport Jazz Festival stars Ella Fitzgerald and Dizzy Gillespie.
Bill Haley and the Comets top the charts with their latest record, 'We're Gonna Rock Around the Clock'.
Elvis Presley records his first song, 'That's All Right Mama'.
William Golding's novel 'Lord of the Flies' is published.

World Events of 1954

Australia's population reaches 9 million.
After 14 years, all rationing ends in the UK.
Colonel Nasser takes power in Egypt and the British give up their occupation.
In Rome, Pope Pius XII warns that television is a potential threat to family life.
Marilyn Monroe marries ex-base baller Joe DiMaggio.
Britain's rabbit population is in danger of being wiped out by the virus myxomatosis.
American evangelist Billy Graham tours Britain.
Queen Elizabeth II is the first reigning monarch to visit Australia.
The McCarthy "witch hunts" begin in the US.
In America, 'Nautilus', the first nuclear submarine, is launched.

Mao Tse-tung is re-elected as leader of China.
The first pre-recorded tapes are available in Britain.
A new board game, Scrabble, is launched.
The Mau-Maus rebel in Kenya.

Sporting Life

American tennis player Maureen Connolly wins her third successive Wimbledon ladies singles title.
British student Roger Bannister is the first man to run a mile in under four minutes in 3 minutes, 59.4 seconds.
24-year-old Australian golfer Peter Thomson becomes the youngest ever winner of the British Open Championship.
British jockey Lester Piggott becomes the youngest Derby winner.

World Events of 1955

Disneyland opens in California, America at a cost of $17m.

Albert Einstein, the scientist, dies at the age of 76.

In the US, Donald Campbell sets a new water speed record of 216.2 mph in his speedboat 'Bluebird'.

'Nautilus', the first nuclear submarine, leaves dock.

James Dean dies in a car accident at the age of 24.

British MPs vote to keep the death penalty.

Germany joins NATO.

Winston Churchill resigns as Prime Minister of Britain and is replaced by Anthony Eden.

In a dispute at Fleet Street, 'The Times' stops publication for the first time in 170 years.

The MacDonalds chain of restaurants is formed in the US.

Civil war breaks out in Vietnam.

Sporting Life

Newcastle United play in a record tenth FA Cup Final, beating Manchester City.

The Grand National is won by Mrs Welman's horse 'Quare Times'.

In tennis, Australia defeat the US to win the Davis Cup.

Louise Brough wins her fourth women's singles championship at Wimbledon.

The first floodlit international football match is played at Wembley, between England and Spain.

In cricket, England defeats Australia 3 tests to 1.

The Arts

Marion Anderson becomes the first black singer to perform at the Metropolitan Opera House, New York.

Tennessee Williams' play 'Cat on a Hot Tin Roof' is premiered in New York.

'Rebel Without a Cause' opens, James Dean's last film.

Hit songs are 'The Yellow Rose of Texas' and 'Sixteen Tons'.

Barry Humphries' character "Edna Everage" makes her stage debut.

Marilyn Monroe stars in 'The Seven Year Itch'.

Right:
The screen idol James Dean made only three films before he was tragically killed in a road accident at the age of 24.

No doubt you have been listening, as I have, to the messages which have been reaching us from all over the world. I always feel that just for these few minutes the march of history stops while we listen to each other, and think of each other, on Christmas Day.

For my husband and myself and for our children, the year that is passing has added to our store of happy memories. We have spent most of it in this country and we have enjoyed seeing many parts of the British Isles which we had not visited before.

Now a New Year will soon be upon us, and we are looking forward to seeing something of Nigeria, that great country in equatorial Africa where more than 30 million of my people have their homes.

For them and for all of us each New Year is an adventure into the unknown. Year by year, new secrets of nature are being revealed to us by science, secrets of immense power for good or evil, according to their use. These discoveries resolve some of our problems, but make others deeper and more immediate.

A hundred years ago our knowledge of the world's surface was by no means complete. To-day most of the blanks have been filled in.

Our new explorations are into new territories of scientific knowledge and into the unknown regions of human behaviour. We have still to solve the problem of living peaceably together as peoples and as nations.

We shall need the faith and determination of our forebears when they crossed uncharted seas into the hidden interiors of Africa and Australia, to guide us on our journeys into the undiscovered realms of the human spirit. In the words of our Poet Laureate:

"Though you have conquered earth and charted sea
And planned the courses of all stars that be
Adventure on, more wonders are in thee
Adventure on, for from the littlest clue
Has come whatever worth man ever knew:
The next to lighten all men may be you."

We must adventure on if we are to make the world a better place. All my peoples of the Commonwealth and Empire have their part to play in this voyage of discovery. We travel all together, just as the Maori tribes sailed all together into the mysterious South Pacific to find New Zealand.

There are certain spiritual values which inspire all of us. We try to express them in our devotion to freedom, which means respect for the individual and equality before the law.

Parliamentary government is also a part of this heritage. We believe in the conception of a Government and opposition and the right to criticise and defend.

All these things are part of the natural life of our free Commonwealth.

Great opportunities lie before us. Indeed a large part of the world looks to the Commonwealth for a lead. We have already gone far towards discovering for ourselves how different nations from North and South, from East and West, can live together in a friendly brotherhood, pooling the resources of each for the benefit of all.

Every one of us can also help in this great adventure. For just as the Commonwealth is made up of different nations, so those nations are made up of individuals. The greater the enterprise, the more important our personal contribution.

The Christmas message to each of us is indivisible: there can be no "peace on earth" without "goodwill toward men."

Scientists talk of "chain reaction" – of power releasing yet more power. This principle must be most true when it is applied to the greatest power of all: the power of love.

My grandfather, King George V, in one of his broadcasts when I was a little girl, called upon his peoples in these words:

"Let each of you be ready and proud to give to his country the service of his work, his mind and his heart."

That is surely the first step to set in motion the "chain reaction" of the powers of light to illuminate the new age ahead of us.

And the second step is this: to understand with sympathy the point of view of others within our own countries and in the Commonwealth as well as those outside it. In this way we can bring our unlimited spiritual resources to bear upon the world.

As this Christmas passes, and time resumes its march, let us resolve that the spirit of Christmas shall stay with us as we journey into the unknown year that lies ahead.

Below:
Sir Winston Churchill, the Prime Minister, holds the door of the royal car open for HM Queen Elizabeth II after she and the Duke of Edinburgh had dined at No 10 Downing Street.

Once again messages of Christmas greeting have been exchanged around the world. From all parts of the Commonwealth, and from the remote and lonely spaces of Antarctica words and thoughts, taking their inspiration from the birth of the Child in Bethlehem long ago, have been carried between us upon the invisible wings of 20th century science.

Neither the long and troubled centuries that have passed since that Child was born, nor the complex scientific developments of our age, have done anything to dim the simple joy and bright hope we all feel when we celebrate His birthday.

That joy and hope find their most complete fulfilment within the loving circle of a united family.

You will understand me, therefore, when I tell you that of all the voices we have heard this afternoon none has given my children and myself greater joy than that of my husband.

To him I say, "From all the members of the family gathered here today our very best good wishes go out to you and to everyone on board 'Britannia' as you voyage together in the far southern seas. Happy Christmas from us, all."

Of course, it is sad for us to be separated on this day, and, of course, we shall look forward to the moment when we shall again be together. Yet my husband's absence at this time has made me even more aware than I was before of my own good fortune in being one of a united family.

With that consciousness in mind, I would like to send a special message of hope and encouragement to all who are not so blessed, or for any reason cannot be with those they love to-day.

To the sick who cannot be at home: to all who serve their country in foreign lands, or whose duty keeps them upon the

Right:
Truro Welcome – On May 10th 1956 schoolchildren wave their flags and cheer as Queen Elizabeth II visits the Cornish capital, Truro.

oceans: and to every man or woman whose destiny it is to walk through life alone.

Particularly on this day of the family festival let us remember those who, like the Holy Family before them, have been driven from their home by war or violence. We call them "refugees".

Let us give them a true refuge: let us see that for them and their children there is room at the inn.

If my husband cannot be at home on Christmas Day, I could not wish for a better reason than that he should be travelling in other parts of the Commonwealth. On his journey, he has returned to many places that we have already visited together, and he has been to others that I have never seen.

On his voyage back to England he will call at some of the least accessible parts of the world, those islands of the South Atlantic separated from us by immense stretches of the ocean, yet linked to us with bonds of brotherhood and trust.

One idea above all others has been the mainspring of this journey: it is the wish to foster and advance concord and understanding within the Commonwealth. No purpose comes nearer to my own desires, for I believe that the way in which our Commonwealth is developing represents one of the most hopeful and imaginative experiments in international affairs that the world has ever seen.

If, as its head, I can make any real personal contribution towards its progress, it must surely be to promote its unity.

We talk of ourselves as a "family of nations" and perhaps our relations, one with another, are not so very different from those which exist between the members of any family. We all know that these are not always easy, for there is no law within a family which binds its members to think, or act, or be alike.

And surely, it is this very freedom of choice and decision which gives exceptional value to friendship in times of stress and disagreement. Such friendship is a gift for which we are often truly and rightly grateful.

None the less, deep and acute differences, involving both intellect and emotion, are bound to arise between members of a family and also between friend and friend, and there is neither virtue nor value in pretending that they do not. In all such differences, however, there comes a moment when for the sake of ultimate harmony the healing power of tolerance, comradeship and love must be allowed to play its part.

I speak of a tolerance that is not indifference, but is rather a willingness to recognise the possibility of right in others: of a comradeship that is not just a sentimental memory of good days past, but the certainty that the tried and staunch friends of yesterday are still in truth the same people to-day: of a love than can rise above anger and is ready to forgive.

That each one of us should give this power a chance to do its work is my heartfelt message to you all upon this Christmas Day. I can think of no better resolve to make nor any better day on which to make it.

Let us remember this during our festivities, for it is part of the Christmas message, "Good will toward men". I wish you all a happy Christmas and a happy New Year.

1956

World Events of 1956

Martin Luther King campaigns for desegregation.

Israel invades Egypt.

Prince Rainier III weds the actress Grace Kelly.

The Suez Crisis between England and Egypt rages.

Soviet troops invade Hungary to quell the revolution.

The US drops the first H-bomb from a plane over Bikini Atoll in the Pacific.

In London, the Duke of Edinburgh announces an award scheme for young people.

Japan joins the United Nations.

The import and export of heroin is banned in Britain.

An oral vaccine against polio is perfected by Dr Albert Sabin in America.

Fidel Castro leads an uprising against the Cuban government.

In the US, the Supreme Court bans segregated bus seating.

In Paris, French Morocco is granted its independence.

Southern Congressmen call on their constituents to resist the Supreme Court ruling against segregation in public schools.

Dwight Eishenhower defeats Adlai Stevenson for US presidency and becomes the first Republican president to win re-election since 1900.

Sporting Life

In cricket, England defeats Australia 2 tests to 1.

The 16th Olympic games opens in Melbourne, Australia.

Jim Laker, the English cricketer, takes 19 wickets in the test against Australia.

British racing driver Stirling Moss wins his second Grand Prix in Monaco.

In football, Real Madrid win the first European Cup.

Lew Hoad beats Ken Rosewall to win the men's singles final at Wimbledon.

The Arts

In London, the National Youth Theatre is founded.

The musical 'My Fair Lady' opens in New York.

John Osborne's new play 'Look Back in Anger' opens.

Eurovision Song Contest is first televised.

Rex Harrison and Julie Andrews star in 'My Fair Lady'.

Hit songs are 'Blue Suede Shoes' and 'Que Sera, Sera'.

Elvis Presley stars in 'Love Me Tender'.

The 'Price is Right' gameshow is broadcast for the first time.

Yul Brynner was sternly majestic in 'The King and I'.

Elvis Presley scores his first Number 1 hit with 'Heartbreak Hotel'.

Left:
On April 19th, American-Irish actress Grace Kelly married Prince Rainier III of Monaco in the clifftop cathedral of St Nicholas, Monaco.
The wedding ceremony was an international media event and was widely televised.

Below and inset:
Hungary was occupied by Soviet troops in 1945, and became a communist country.
In October 1956 the communists were overthrown in a revolution, but this was quickly thwarted when the Soviet army invaded the country again and it was restored to communist rule.

1957

Right:
Harold Macmillan becomes new Prime Minister.

Below left:
Sputnik-2 saw the launch of the first dog, Laika, into space.

Below right:
The film 'The Bridge on the River Kwai', starred Sir Alec Guinness.

World Events of 1957

2,000 people a week are reported to be emigrating from the UK to the Commonwealth.

In Pretoria, South Africa drops 'God Save the Queen' as its national anthem.

The Gold Coast is granted its independence, and renamed Ghana.

In America, San Francisco is hit by the worst tremors since the great earthquake of 1906.

A tidal wave and hurricane kills over 500 people in Louisana and Texas.

Britain conducts its first nuclear weapon tests in Western Australia.

Harold Macmillan becomes the new Prime Minister of Britain.

The European Common Market, to become the European Economic Community (EEC), is created.

Russia launches Sputnik-I, the first space satellite, this was followed with the launch of Sputnik-2 with a dog, Laika, on board.

Elvis Presley is called up to join the army.

The world's longest suspension bridge, the Mackinac Straits Bridge, Michigan is constructed.

The Asian Flu epidemic breaks out in Australia.

Olaf V becomes the King of Norway.

Dr Jonas Salk's polio vaccine proves effective in fighting polio by cutting incidences of the disease by 80 percent.

The Calentano Brothers introduced the first-ever frozen pizza on to the market and started a convenience food revolution.

Frisbee-craze: these aerodynamic plastic disks put a new spin on the game of catch.

For the first time ever, the US Surgeon General reports a link between cigarette smoking and lung cancer.

In the desert outside Las Vegas, the US Atomic Energy Commission detonates the first underground atomic blast.

Sporting Life

In football, Real Madrid win the European Cup Final.

American Althea Gibson becomes the first black Wimbledon champion.

The Australian Soccer Federation is founded.

In tennis, Australia beats the US to win the Davis Cup.

In Britain, the Grand National is won by 'Sundew'.

The Arts

'The Bridge on the River Kwai' wins Oscars

Marilyn Monroe stars in 'The Prince and the Showgirl'.

French novelist Albert Camus wins the Nobel Prize for Literature.

The Royal Ballet is founded.

With its 1,998th performance, Agatha Christie's 'The Mousetrap' becomes Britain's longest-running play.

Hit songs are 'Maria' and 'Love Letters in the Sand'.

'Perry Mason', starring Raymond Burr as a methodical lawyer, is the most popular TV series.

Rock Hudson and Kim Novak are the two most popular Hollywood stars.

Happy Christmas. Twenty-five years ago my grandfather broadcast the first of these Christmas messages. Today is another landmark because television has made it possible for many of you to see me in your homes on Christmas Day. My own family often gather round to watch television, as they are at this moment, and that is how I imagine you now.

I very much hope that this new medium will make my Christmas message more personal and direct. It is inevitable that I should seem a rather remote figure to many of you – a successor to the kings and queens of history: someone whose face may be familiar in newspapers and films but who never really touches your personal lives. But now, at least for a few minutes, I welcome you to the peace of my own home.

That it is possible for some of you to see me today is just another example of the speed at which things are changing all around us. Because of these changes I am not surprised that many people feel lost and unable to decide what to hold on to and what to discard, how to take advantage of the new life without losing the best of the old.

But it is not the new inventions which are the difficulty. The trouble is caused by unthinking people who carelessly throw away ageless ideals as if they were old and outworn machinery. They would have religion thrown aside, morality in personal and public life made meaningless, honesty counted as foolishness, and self-interest set up in place of self-restraint.

At this critical moment in our history we will certainly lose the trust and respect of the world if we just abandon those fundamental principles which guided the men and women who built the greatness of this country and

Commonwealth. Today we need a special kind of courage, not the kind needed in battle, but a kind which makes us stand up for everything that we know is right, everything that is true and honest. We need the kind of courage that can withstand the subtle corruption of the cynics, so that we can show the world that we are not afraid of the future.

It has always been easy to hate and destroy. To build and to cherish is much more difficult. That is why we can take a pride in the new Commonwealth we are building. This year Ghana and Malaya joined our brotherhood. Both these countries are now entirely self-governing. Both achieved their new status amicably and peacefully.

This advance is a wonderful tribute to the efforts of men of good will who have worked together as friends, and I welcome these two countries with all my heart.

Last October I opened the new Canadian Parliament, and, as you know, this was the first time that any sovereign had done so in Ottawa. Once again I was overwhelmed by the loyalty and enthusiasm of my Canadian people.

Also during 1957 my husband and I paid visits to Portugal, France, Denmark, and the United States of America. In each case the arrangements and formalities were managed with great skill, but no one could have "managed" the welcome we received from the people.

In each country I was welcomed as head of the Commonwealth and as your representative. These nations are our friends largely because we have always tried to do our best to be honest and kindly and because we have tried to stand up for what we believe to be right.

In the old days the monarch led his soldiers on the battlefield and his leadership at all times was close and

personal. Today things are very different. I cannot lead you into battle. I do not give you laws or administer justice. But I can do something else. I can give you my heart and my devotion to these old islands and to all the peoples of our brotherhood of nations.

I believe in our qualities and in our strength. I believe that together we can set an example to the world which will encourage upright people everywhere.

I would like to read you a few lines from 'Pilgrim's Progress', because I am sure we can say with Mr. Valiant for Truth, these words: "Though with great difficulty I am got hither, yet now I do not repent me of all the trouble I have been at to arrive where I am. My sword I give to him that shall succeed me in my pilgrimage and my courage and skill to him that can get it. My marks and scars I carry with me to be witness for me that I have fought his battles who now will be my rewarder."

I hope that 1958 may bring you God's blessing and all the things you long for. And so I wish you all, young and old, wherever you may be, all the fun and enjoyment and the peace of a very happy Christmas.

Below:
Queen Elizabeth driving with her children at Windsor.

1958

World Events of 1958

Charles de Gaulle is elected President of France.

Queen Elizabeth II opens Gatwick Airport in England.

The world's largest oil tanker, capable of carrying 1,021,000 barrels, is launched in Japan.

The first radar speed checks are used in London.

The Campaign for Nuclear Disarmament (CND) is founded.

The Hovercraft is invented.

Unemployment in the US reaches 5 million.

In Stockholm, Dr Ake Senning implants the first internal heart pace maker.

Krushchev becomes the Soviet Prime Minister.

America launches the first moon rocket.

Prince Charles becomes the Prince of Wales.

Britain's first motorway opens.

Race riots flare in Notting Hill Gate, London.

US launches its first satellite 'Explorer 1' into orbit in January, followed by a frantic launch programme to recapture ground lost to the Russians.

Left:
General Charles de Gaulle took over from Pierre Pflimlin as Prime Minister of France on June 1st, 1958.

Below left:
In February a new pressure group, CND (The Campaign for Nuclear Disarmament), was launched under the presidency of the philosopher and peace campaigner Bertrand Russell.

Sporting Life

Seven Manchester United footballers are killed in the Munich plane crash.

Pakistan's cricket team visits the West Indies for the first time.

In cricket, Australia defeats South Africa 3 tests to nil.

The Grand National is won by 'Mr What'.

In football, Bolton Wanderers beat Manchester United to win the FA Cup.

Hula Hoop hype sweeps America, then the world: seventy million were sold during the year.

The world's first skateboard is invented in California by attaching rollerskate wheels to a square board.

The Arts

'The Bridge on the River Kwai' wins three British Academy Awards.

Boris Pasternak wins the Nobel Prize for Literature and publishes his novel 'Dr Zhivago'.

Hit songs are 'Magic Moments' and 'All I Have to do is Dream'.

The film 'Gigi' wins nine Oscars.

David Niven receives the Academy Award for Best Actor for his performance in 'Seperate Tables'.

'High Fidelity' is the big buzzphrase in the music industry with the introduction of the stereophonic LP.

Elizabeth Taylor stars as Maggie (with Paul Newman as the male lead) in Tennessee Williams 'Cat on a Hot Tin Roof'.

Miles Davis forms his renowned sextet in New York with John Coltrane, Cannonball Adderly, Bill Evans, Paul Chambers and Philly Joe Jones: widely considered to be his best band.

Duke Ellington was the hit of the Newport Jazz Festival with his Jazz suite 'Black, Brown and Beige'.

A happy Christmas to you all Every year I look forward to opening the letters, parcels and telegrams that come to me from all parts of the world. My husband and children join me in thanking all of you who have sent us your good wishes for Christmas and the New Year.

Some of you have written to say that you would like to see our children on television this afternoon. We value your interest in them and I can assure you that we have thought about this a great deal before deciding against it. We would like our son and daughter to grow up as normally as possible so that they will be able to serve you and the Commonwealth faithfully and well when they are old enough to do so. We believe that public life is not a fair burden to place on growing children. I'm sure that all of you who are parents will understand.

Very soon now we shall be entering into the uncertainty and promise of a new year. I hope very much that it proves to be a year of progress and happiness for us all.

Below:
Pat Boone singer and actor with Ron Parry and Antonio the dancer meet Queen Elizabeth II at the variety show at the Coliseum.

My family and I are looking forward to it, especially because many of us will be travelling to different parts of the world and hope to see more of you than ever before.

In three weeks' time my husband goes to India and Pakistan and then on across the Pacific. My mother is going to East Africa and my uncle, the Duke of Gloucester, and his wife will be travelling as my representatives to Nigeria.

My aunt, the Duchess of Kent, and my cousin, Princess Alexandra, are also undertaking long journeys. Together they will be visiting Central and South America in the spring, and later Princess Alexandra goes to Australia to attend the centenary celebrations of the State of Queensland.

In June my husband and I will be going to Canada once again. You'll remember that my sister, Princess Margaret, was there earlier this year. This time we go primarily to open the great St Lawrence Seaway, but we shall be visiting many other parts of the country as well.

Lastly – towards the end of the year – we are going to Ghana and on our way back we intend to visit my people in Sierra Leone and the Gambia.

So, between us, we are going to many parts of the world. We have no plans for space travel – at the moment.

To Christians all over the world Christmas is an occasion for family gatherings and celebrations, for presents and parties, for friendship and good will. To many of my people Christmas doesn't have the same religious significance, but friendship and good will are common to us all. So it's a good time to remember those around us who are far from home, feeling perhaps strange and lonely.

My own thoughts are with the men and women and children from other parts of the Commonwealth who have come to live and work in the great cities of this country and may well be missing the warmth and sunshine of their homelands.

In recent years the Commonwealth countries have been making a great co-operative effort to raise standards of living. Even so, the pace of our everyday life has been such that there has hardly been enough time to enjoy the things which appeal to men's minds and which make life a full experience. After all, our standard of living has a spiritual as well as a material aspect. The genius of scientists, inventors, and engineers can make life more comfortable and prosperous. But throughout history the spiritual and intellectual aspirations of mankind have been inspired by prophets and dreamers, philosophers, men of ideas and poets, artists in paint, sculpture, and music, the whole company who challenge and encourage or who entertain and give pleasure.

To their number I would add the teachers in church, school, and university, whose enormous job it is to awaken the minds of the younger generations and instil into them the essence of our accumulated civilization.

I am sure that many of you have thought about these things before, but it seems to me that Christmas is just the time to be grateful to those who add fullness to our lives.

Even so, we need something more. We all need the kind of security that one gets from a happy and united family. Before I return to mine let me once again wish every one of you a very happy Christmas from all of us here at Sandringham, and may God's blessing be with you in the coming year.

1959

World Events of 1959

Britain recognises Fidel Castro as leader of a new government in Cuba.

Rock singer Buddy Holly dies in a plane crash.

The first section of the London – Birmingham motorway (M1) opens.

In France, work begins on a road tunnel beneath Mont Blanc.

Britain and Iceland are engaged in a "Cod War".

In the US, the state of Alabama bans a children's book because it shows a black rabbit marrying a white one.

Cinema attendances drop in the UK as TV booms.

In the UK, the number of people going to University has doubled since 1939.

In an international treaty, 12 countries agree to preserve the Antarctic as a science reserve.

Alaska becomes 49th US state and six months later Hawaii is proclaimed 50th US state.

'Vanguard 2' the first US weather satellite is launched into space.

Vice-President Richard Nixon visits Russia and warns the country it "will live in tension and fear" if it attempts to spread communism beyond its borders.

Russian Premier Nikita Kruschev visits the US: he enjoys hot dogs, but is outraged when told he cannot visit Disneyland for "security reasons".

Sporting Life

In football, Nottingham Forest beat Luton Town 2 – 1 to win the FA Cup Final.

In cricket, Australia defeats England 4 tests to nil.

Golfer Jack Nicklaus wins the USGA Amateur title.

In tennis, Australia wins the Davis Cup against the US.

British racing driver Stirling Moss wins the Italian Grand Prix.

The Arts

A work of art by Picasso is sold for £55,000, a world-record for a living artist.

The film 'Ben Hur' opens in Britain and Australia.

Hit songs are 'What do you Want to Make those Eyes at me For?' and 'Livin' Doll'.

D.H. Lawrence's book "Lady Chatterley's Lover" is banned in the US.

Actor David Niven wins an Oscar.

Barbie dolls make a rather shaky debut, judged too "developed" for a young girl's doll.

"Phone-booth packing", the art of seeing just how many people you can fit into a phone booth, becomes the rage.

George Reeves, the former star of 'Superman' dies in apparently mysterious circumstances not having worked for over two years.

Rock Hudson and Doris Day starred together in the popular romantic farce 'Pillow Talk'.

Below:
Buddy Holly, with his band, The Crickets, created a sensational new sound in popular music and made a major contribution to the birth of a teen culture in the West. His songs were recorded by other artists and strongly influenced The Beatles. He died in a plane crash in 1959 during a punishing tour of concerts.

FIRST OCCASION

It was the first occasion during her reign on which the Queen's Christmas message was broadcast from a recording made in advance.

A BBC spokesman said there had not been one complaint of bad reception of the speech.

Christmas Day at Sandringham for the Royal Family began with worship. After attending Holy Communion at the parish church, the Queen and other members of the Royal Family returned for morning service at 11am.

Left:
Queen Elizabeth II and Prince Philip, Duke of Edinburgh with their children Charles, Prince of Wales and Princess Anne, by a cannon of a bygone age on the East Terrace of Windsor Castle, Berkshire.

Below:
Queen Elizabeth II with her husband Prince Philip, the Duke of Edinburgh.

The Queen's Christmas message – recorded in advance and this year appreciably shorter than in the past – was broadcast throughout the Commonwealth on Christmas Day.

The Queen was at Sandringham. In addition to the Duke of Edinburgh and the Prince of Wales and Princess Anne, the Queen Mother and Princess Margaret, the Royal Family Christmas party there included the Duke and Duchess of Gloucester and their children, Prince William and Prince Richard, and the Duchess of Kent, Princess Alexandra and Prince Michael.

The text of the message, which the Queen recorded in her study at Buckingham Palace on December 17, and which lasted about one minute was:

I do not want Christmas to pass by without sending my best wishes for a happy day to all of you who may be listening, and especially to my own peoples in the Commonwealth.

Wherever you are and whatever you may be doing, you have my constant interest and affection.

I am particularly grateful to the many kind people over the world who have sent me their good wishes at this time. I am glad to have this chance to thank you all warmly indeed.

As the old year passes, let us celebrate Christmas with thanksgiving and carry its message of peace and good will into the year ahead.

All of us at Sandringham wish you a very happy Christmas.

May God bless you all.

Right:
Queen Elizabeth II with her only daughter and second child, Princess Anne arm-in-arm in the gardens of Windsor Castle.

I am glad at Christmas time to have this opportunity of speaking directly to all the peoples of the Commonwealth and of sending you my good wishes. My husband and our children, together with the other members of our family, join me in wishing every one of you a happy Christmas and a prosperous New Year.

I make no excuse for telling you once again that the kind messages which reach us from all over the world at this season give us great pleasure and encouragement. This year I was delighted to get so many when my second son was born. The telegrams and letters, which came flooding in at that time made me feel very close to all the family groups throughout the Commonwealth.

It is this feeling of personal association which gives the peoples of the Commonwealth countries that special relationship, one to another, which others find so difficult to understand. It is because of this that my husband and I are so greatly looking forward to our visits to India and Pakistan early next year and later on to Ghana, Sierra Leone and the Gambia.

By no stretch of the imagination can 1960 be described as a happy or successful year for mankind. Arguments and strained relations as well as natural disasters have all helped to produce an atmosphere of tension and uncertainty all over the world.

Although the causes are beyond the control of individuals, we can at least influence the future by our everyday behaviour. It is at times of change, disorder and uncertainty that we should cling most strongly to all those principles which we know to be right and good.

Civilization as we know it, or would like it to be, depends upon a constant striving towards better things. In times of stress, such as we are living through, only a determined effort by men and women of good will everywhere can halt and reverse a growing tendency towards violence and disintegration.

Despite the difficulties there are encouraging signs. For instance, in Africa, Nigeria has gone through the process of achieving full self-government in peace and good will. This great nation of 30 million people has decided to remain a member of our Commonwealth and I know that her influence will be most valuable as the future unfolds in other parts of Africa.

Then again, cooperation between Commonwealth countries grows every year and the understanding and mutual appreciation which is developing at the same time is one of the really bright spots in the world today.

Although the contribution which any one person can make is small, it is real and important. Whether you live in one of the rapidly developing countries of the Commonwealth or whether you find yourself in one of the older countries, the work of mutual help and the increase of mutual understanding cannot fail to be personally satisfying and of real service to the future.

May the months ahead bring you joy and the peace and happiness which we so much desire.

Happy Christmas; God bless you all.

1960

World Events of 1960

The actor Clark Gable dies.

The population of the US is nearly 180 million.

Mrs Bandaranaike becomes Prime Minister of Ceylon, the world's first woman Prime Minister.

Australian aborigines become Australian Citizens and are eligible for Social Service benefits.

The first weather satellite is launched by the US.

John Fitzgerald Kennedy becomes the President of the US.

The Congo is given its independence.

In Britain, 200,000 copies of 'Lady Chatterley's Lover' D.H. Lawrence, sell out in one day.

National Service ends in Britain.

In Johannesburg, South Africa, all black political organisations are banned.

Cyprus claims its independence from Britain.

Women ministers are accepted for the first time by the Swedish Church.

Leonid Brezhnev becomes Soviet President.

The laser beam is invented.

Sporting Life

The Olympic Games open in Rome.

16-year-old Bobby Fischer successfully defends the US chess crown.

In tennis, Australia defeats Spain to win the Davis Cup.

In football, Real Madrid win the European Cup for the fifth time in a row.

US boxers, including Cassius Clay win three gold medals in the Olympics.

The Arts

The film 'Psycho' opens.

Hit songs are 'Let's Do the Twist' and 'It's an Itsy Bitsy Teeny Weeny Yellow Polka Dot Bikini'.

'Ben Hur' starring Charlton Heston wins a record 10 Oscars.

The Royal Shakespeare Company is inaugurated in Britain.

Left:
John F Kennedy was elected US President in 1960. In his inaugural address he said, "Ask not what your country can do for you – ask what can you do for your country?"

1961

World Events of 1961

The millionth Morris Minor is produced.

Britain applies to join the Common Market.

The Orient Express runs from Paris to Bucharest for the last time.

Soviet cosmonaut Yuri Gagarin becomes the first man in space.

The Bay of Pigs in Cuba is invaded.

Fossil bones are discovered in Africa, said to push the origins of humans back millions of years.

The first pay-phones are installed in the UK.

Russian ballet dancer Rudolf Nureyev defects to the West.

The contraceptive pill goes on sale in the UK and Australia.

John F. Kennedy is sworn in as the youngest President of the US.

The construction of the Berlin Wall begins.

Malta gains independence from Britain.

In Rabat, Hassan II becomes King of Morocco, on the death of King Mohammed V.

South Africa becomes a republic and leaves the Commonwealth.

The earliest surviving mosaics in Britain are discovered at Fishbourne.

Sporting Life

In tennis, Australia beats Italy 5 games to nil to win the Davis Cup.

South African golfer Gary Player wins the US Masters by a single stroke.

At Wimbledon, Australian Rod Laver wins the men's singles final.

In Monaco, Stirling Moss wins the Monaco Grand Prix.

The Arts

Marlene Dietrich stars in 'Judgment at Nuremburg'.

Walt Disney's '101 Dalmatins' is released.

Hit songs are 'Wooden Heart' and "You Don't Know".

American novelist Ernest Hemingway commits suicide.

In the UK, the Shakespeare Memorial Theatre at Stratford-on-Avon becomes the Royal Shakespeare Theatre.

"Pop Art", a new art movement, becomes popular.

Above left:
On April 12 1961 the Soviet Union put the first man into space. Major Yuri Gagarin, 27, orbited the earth and made a safe return. He reportedly told the Soviet premier Kruschev, "I could see seas, mountains, big cities, rivers and forests".

Right:
The celebrated dancer Rudolf Nureyev was granted political asylum in Paris after making a dash for freedom from the Soviet "minders" accompanying the Kirov Ballet just as they were leaving for London. He was one of the greatest ballet dancers of all time.

Right:
Queen Elizabeth II in the Throne Room of the Vatican with Pope John XXIII (1881 – 1963), Angelo Guiseppe Roncalli, who is reading his welcome address.

Below:
Queen Elizabeth II of Great Britain enjoying an elephant ride at Benares during a tour of India.

Every year at this time the whole Christian world celebrates the birth of the founder of our faith. It is traditionally the time for family reunions, present-giving and children's parties. A welcome escape, in fact, from the harsh realities of this troubled world, and it is just in times like these, times of tensions and anxieties, that the simple story and message of Christmas is most relevant.

The story is of a poor man and his wife who took refuge at night in a stable, where a child was born and laid in the manger. Nothing very spectacular, and yet the event was greeted with that triumphant song – "Glory to God in the highest, and on earth peace, good will towards men". For that child was to show that there is nothing in heaven and earth that cannot be achieved by faith and by love and service to one's neighbour. Christmas may be a Christian festival, but its message goes out to all men and it is echoed by all men of understanding and goodwill everywhere.

During this last year I have been able to visit many countries: some were members of the Commonwealth and some were not. In all of them I was shown a genuine kindness and affection which touched me deeply and showed, I think, that the British people are looked upon as friends in many parts of the world.

In Asia and in Africa we were made aware of the great volume of goodwill and friendship that exists between all the varied peoples who profess different faiths and who make up our Commonwealth family. To them their Christian brethren send a message of hope and encouragement this Christmas.

It goes also to the quiet people who fight prejudice by example, who stick to standards and ideals in face of persecution: who make real sacrifices in order to help and serve their neighbours.

"Oh hush the noise, ye men of strife, and hear the angels sing." The words of this old carol mean even more today than when they were first written.

We can only dispel the clouds of anxiety by the patient and determined efforts of us all. It cannot be done by condemning the past or by contracting out of the present. Angry words and accusations certainly don't do any good, however justified they may be.

It is natural that the younger generation should lose patience with their elders, for their seeming failure to bring some order and security to the world, but things will not get any better if young people merely express themselves by indifference or by revulsion against what they regard as an out-of-date order of things.

The world desperately needs their vigour, their determination, and their service to their fellow-men. The opportunities are there and the reward is the satisfaction of truly unselfish work.

To both young and old I send my very best wishes, and, as the carol says, may we all hear the angels sing in the coming year.

A very happy Christmas to you all.

A merry Christmas and a Happy New Year.

There is something wonderful in the way these old familiar warm-hearted words of the traditional Christmas message never seem to grow stale. Surely it is because the family festival is like a firm landmark in the stormy seas of modern life.

Year by year, our families change and grow up. So does our Commonwealth family. This year Jamaica, Trinidad and Tobago and Uganda have joined the circle as full members and we wish them all good fortune.

My husband and I are greatly looking forward to re-visiting New Zealand and Australia in the New Year. We shall meet many old friends and make new ones and we shall be very interested to see some of the many new developments which have taken place since I was last there nine years ago.

In spite of all the changes of the modern world and the many stresses and strains involved, the feeling of a special relationship between the ordinary people of the older Commonwealth countries will never be weakened. This feeling is rapidly spreading throughout the newer members and in its turn will help us to realise the ideal of human brotherhood.

In the ideal of the Commonwealth we have been entrusted with something very special. We have in our hands a most potent force for good, and one of the true unifying bonds in this torn world. Let us keep faith with the ideal we know to be right and be ambitious for the good of all men.

Mankind continues to achieve wonders in technical and space research but in the Western world perhaps the launching of 'Telstar' has captured the imagination most vividly.

Left:
Queen Elizabeth II talks to some of the Chelsea Pensioners at the Royal Hospital's Founder's Day Parade in London.

This tiny satellite has become the invisible focus of a million eyes.

Telstar, and her sister satellites as they arise, can now show the world to the world just as it is in its daily life. What a wonderfully exciting prospect, and perhaps it will make us stop and think about what sort of picture we are presenting to each other.

Wise men since the beginning of time have studied the skies. Whatever our faith, we can all follow a star – indeed we must follow one if the immensity of the future opening before us is not to dazzle our eyes and dissipate our sense of direction.

How is it, people wonder, that we are for ever seeking new worlds to conquer before we have properly put our own house in order?

Some people are uncertain which star to follow, or if any star is worth following at all. What is it all for, they ask, if you can bounce a telephone conversation, or a television picture through the skies and across the world, yet still find lonely people living in the same street?

Following a star has many meanings: It can mean the religious man's approach to God or the hopes of parents for their children, or the ambition of young men and women, or the devotion of old countries like ours to well-tried ideals of toleration and justice, with no distinction of race or creed.

The wise men of old followed a star. Modern man has built one. But unless the message of this new star is the same as theirs our wisdom will count for nought. Now we can all say "the world is my neighbour" and it is only in serving one another that we can reach for the stars.

God bless you all.

1962

World Events of 1962

Marilyn Monroe dies.

There is an outbreak of smallpox in Britain.

John Glenn is the first American to orbit the earth.

The world's population is more than 3 billion.

Amnesty International is created.

The Cuban missile crisis sees the world on the brink of a nuclear war.

In Australia, Aborigines are granted the right to vote.

"The Twist" is the latest dance craze.

Jamaica, Trinidad and Tobago are granted their independence.

French leader Charles de Gaulle survives an assassination attempt.

In Stockholm, Sweden, two sisters who are married to two brothers, give birth in the same hospital on the same day.

In London, share values fall by £1,000 million, the biggest slump since 1929.

In San Francisco, three prisoners dig their way out of Alcatraz using spoons.

In Washingon, the Supreme Court bans "official prayers" in schools.

Sporting Life

The Commonwealth games open in Perth, Australia.

In football, Brazil win the World Cup.

Australian tennis player Rod Laver becomes the first Australian to win the Grand Slam.

Australia wins a record 38 Commonwealth Games gold medals.

In Karachi, England cricketers win the Test series against Pakistan.

The Arts

Elizabeth Taylor and Richard Burton star in 'Cleopatra'.

"Pop Art" by Andy Warhol and Roy Lichtenstein is all the rage.

'A Clockwork Orange', a novel by Anthony Burgess, is published.

The film 'Lawrence of Arabia' is released.

Hit songs are 'I Remember You' and 'Blowin' in the Wind'.

John Steinbeck wins the Nobel Prize for Literature.

Left:
Marilyn Monroe made 23 films and became the ultimate sex symbol. Her life was lonely and troubled and she was found dead in her bed with an empty bottle of sleeping pills on the bedside table.

1963

Britain is refused entry into the EEC.
Khrushchev warns that a nuclear war
would kill 800 million people.
The Americans, Soviets and British
sign a nuclear test ban.
The Great Train Robbery takes place.
Kenya gains its independence.
In Britain, the BBC ends its ban on
mentioning royalty, politics, religion
and sex in its comedy shows.
A 50 mph speed limit is introduced
in the UK, but ignored by most drivers.
A "hot-line" between the White
House and the Kremlin is introduced.
A new island is created off the south
coast of Iceland, following volcanic
activity on the ocean floor.

Sporting Life

Football team Tottenham become
the first British team to win the
European Cup Winners Cup.
Athlete Bob Hayes runs 100 yards in
a record 9.1 seconds.
Margaret Smith is the first Australian
woman to win Wimbledon.
In cricket, the West Indies win the
Test series against England.
Boxer Sonny Liston successfully
defends his heavyweight crown.

The Arts

The Beatles record their first LP
'Please Please Me'.
'Lawrence of Arabia' wins seven
Oscars.
Alfred Hitchcock's film 'The Birds' is
released.
Hit songs are 'She Loves You' and
'From Me to You'.
The James Bond movie 'From
Russia With Love' is released.

Right:
President Kennedy
supported the Civil
Rights movement,
but its greatest
hero was Martin
Luther King. In a
famous speech he
said, "I have a
dream that one day
this nation will rise
up and live out the
true meaning of its
creed: 'We hold
these truths to be
self-evident, that
all men are
created equal'."

Above:
It is said that everyone alive at the time remembers
exactly where they were, whom they were with and
what they were doing when they heard the tragic news
that President John F Kennedy had been shot dead in
Dallas on November 22nd. The whole world mourned
a much loved and admired President.

World Events of 1963

John F. Kennedy is assassinated in
Dallas.
Martin Luther King leads 200,000 in
a civil rights march.
The Profumo scandal rocks the
British government.
In Canada, archaeologists find Viking
remains dating from 500 years
before Columbus's arrival in America.

Since my last message of Christmas greetings to you all the world has witnessed many great events and sweeping changes, but they are already part of the long record of history. Now, as ever, the important time for mankind is the future. The coming years are full of hope and promise and their course can still be shaped by our will and action.

The Christmas message of peace on earth, goodwill toward men, remains the same; but we can only achieve this if we are all truly ambitious for what is good and honourable. Humanity can only make progress by determination and concerted effort.

One such concerted effort has been the campaign to free the world from hunger. I am very happy to know that the people of the Commonwealth have responded so generously to this campaign. Much has been achieved but there is still much to do and on this day of reunions and festivities in the glow of Christmas, let us remember the many undernourished people, young and old, scattered throughout the world.

All my family joins me in sending every one of you best wishes for Christmas and may God's blessing be with you in the coming year.

Above:
Noel Cantwell of Manchester United receives the FA Cup 1963, presented by Queen Elizabeth II and Prince Philip after winning the final against Leicester City at Wembley.

Left:
Queen Elizabeth II in Ghana, West Africa.

Right:
Queen Elizabeth II, Prince Philip, Prince Andrew and Prince Edward waving to the crowds from the balcony at Buckingham Palace, during the Trooping of the Colour.

As I begin my Christmas broadcast to you, the people of Great Britain and of the other Commonwealth countries, my mind travels far away, and for one moment I seem to be with you in many countries, which are now almost as familiar as my own native land.

To you all, my family and I send our affectionate greetings and hope that your Christmas is a happy one.

Let us think for a moment about this great Commonwealth. What is this wealth which we have in common and which is so much more than our collective resources, massive though they are?

I know that life is hard for many. The problems which face mankind often seem to defy solution. Some of our Commonwealth friends overseas are grappling with difficulties unknown in a complex industrial country such as Great Britain. There are difficulties of over population, there is hunger, and drought and lack of power. There are yearly tens of thousands of young people flocking into schools, seeking education.

I welcome the chance of hearing more about these problems when individual Ministers from the Commonwealth come to this country, and also on such special occasions as the Prime Ministers' meetings. At moments like this I have the benefit, not only of getting to know some of my Prime Ministers better, but of welcoming leaders from the new nations of the Commonwealth.

I value very highly these meetings, which allow me to draw on the wisdom of such a representative gathering. I believe that in God's good time all the peoples of our Commonwealth, working side by side, will attain prosperity.

The thread which runs through our Commonwealth is love of freedom, and it is perhaps in this, more than in anything else, that our real wealth lies. Now the word "freedom", like the word "democracy" is a simple one implying a simple idea, and yet freedom, to be effective, must be disciplined.

Absolute freedom is a state unknown to the historian. The many ancient institutions and traditions which we have inherited and which are familiar to us all, provide a framework and a dignified background to our way of life.

If it is not to degenerate, freedom must be maintained by a thousand invisible forces, self-discipline, the common law, the right of citizens to assemble, and to speak and argue. We do not wish to impose a particular form of government on any peoples in the world: we merely say "this is what we do: we know it's not perfect, but it is the best system that we have been able to create after many centuries of trial and error".

All of us who have been blessed with young families know from long experience that when one's house is at its noisiest, there is often less cause for anxiety. The creaking of a ship in a heavy sea is music in the ears of the captain on the bridge. In fact little is static and without movement there can be no progress.

Some speak today as though the age of adventure and initiative is past. On the contrary, never have the challenges been greater or more urgent. The fight against poverty, malnutrition and ignorance is harder than ever, and we must do all in our power to see that science is directed towards solving these problems.

I would like to say one more word to the young people of the Commonwealth. Upon you rests our hope for the future. You young people are needed: there is a great task ahead of you – the building of a new world. You have brains and courage, imagination and humanity: direct them to the things that have to be achieved in this century, if mankind is to live together in happiness and prosperity.

God bless you and a very, very happy Christmas to you all.

1964

World Events of 1964

Harold Wilson becomes the Prime Minister of Britain.
Beatlemania sweeps through the US.
The United Nations sends a peace-keeping force to Cyprus.
The US bombs North Vietnam.
In South Africa, Nelson Mandela is sentenced to life imprisonment.
Race riots break out in Harlem, New York.
Dr Martin Luther King is awarded the Nobel Peace Prize.
Krushchev is ousted in USSR and Brezhnev and Kosygin rise to power.
Topless swimsuits appear in the south of France.
In Northern Rhodesia, Kenneth Kaunda, the nation's first premier, is sworn in.
£10 notes are issued for the first time in the UK since World War II.
France and Britain agree to construct a Channel Tunnel costing £160 million.
In Jerusalem, the Palestine Liberation Organisation is created.
Europe's longest bridge, the Forth Road Bridge, opens in the UK.

Sporting Life

The Olympic Games are held in Tokyo.
In British football, West Ham win the FA Cup Final.
Boxer Cassius Clay wins the heavy-weight championship of the world.
Dawn Fraser wins her 8th Olympic medal – an Australian record.
In cricket, Australia draw the test series with South Africa.
South Africa is banned from the Olympics for apartheid policies.

The Arts

'Fiddler on the Roof' opens on Broadway.
Julie Andrews stars in 'Mary Poppins'.
Ernest Hemingway's novel 'A Moveable Feast' is published.
Hit songs are 'I Love You Because' and 'It's Over'.
The film 'The Pink Panther' opens starring Peter Sellers.
Sidney Poitier becomes the first black to win an Oscar, for best actor in 'Lilies of the Field'.
French novelist Jean-Paul Sartre rejects a Nobel Prize.
'The Great Escape' is released.

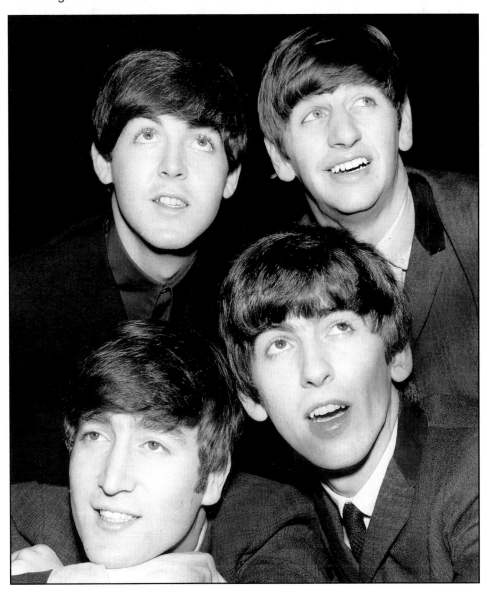

Left:
John, Paul, George and Ringo were pursued by thousands of screaming fans at airports and concerts, giving rise to a new phenomenon in pop music. The Beatles first appeared in the United States in 1964 on the Ed Sullivan Show.

1965

World Events of 1965

American Edward White is the first astronaut to walk in space.

Malcolm X, Black Muslim leader, is assassinated in New York.

In Britain, the death penalty is abolished.

Sir Winston Churchill dies.

The Beatles are awarded MBEs.

The first woman High Court judge, Judge Elizabeth Lane is appointed in Britain.

The US suffers its biggest power cut in American history when New York City and parts of nine states are blacked out.

United Nations Children's Fund (UNICEF) is awarded the Nobel Peace Prize.

Guerrilla leader Che Guevara leaves Cuba.

The first Japanese cars are imported to the UK.

Lyndon B. Johnson is sworn in as the new President of the US.

A violent cyclone in East Pakistan kills over 10,000.

Below: Gary Player, winner of the US Open Golf Championship.

The state of New York abolishes the death sentence.

In the US, Yale University claims that a 1440 map proves that the Vikings discovered North America.

Sporting Life

Gary Player wins the US Open Golf championship. Jack Nicklaus wins the Masters.

12-year-old South African Karen Muir swims 110 yards backstroke in a world record 68.7 seconds.

In English football, Liverpool beat Leeds United to win the FA Cup Final for the first time.

Boxer Cassius Clay beats Sonny Liston for the world title.

In cricket, the West Indies defeats Australia 2 tests to 1.

The Arts

The Seekers 'I'll Never Find Another You' is the first Australian record to sell one million copies.

The Rolling Stones have three number one hits in Britain.

'The Sound of Music' wins an Academy Award.

Hit songs are 'A Hard Day's Night' and 'A Walk in the Black Forest'.

The Beatles star in the film 'Help!'.

Above:
The British nation and the world mourned the century's greatest leader. Thousands queued day and night to file past Winston Churchill's bier as he lay in state in Westminster Hall, and tributes poured in from around the globe.

Right:
Cheering Ethiopians line the route as Queen Elizabeth II and President Dr El Tieani El Mahi drive past in an open car during a royal tour of Sudan.

Below:
Queen Elizabeth II and Prince Philip with Jackie Kennedy and her children John Jr (1960 – 1999) and Caroline during the inauguration of Britain's Kennedy memorial at Runnymede.

Every year the familiar pattern of Christmas unfolds. The sights and the customs and festivities may seem very much the same from one year to another; and yet to families and individuals each Christmas is slightly different. Children grow and presents for them change.

It may be the first Christmas for many as husband and wife. Or the first Christmas with grandchildren. Some may be far from home and others lonely or sick. Yet Christmas always remains as the great family festival, a festival which we owe to that family long ago which spent this time in extreme adversity and discomfort.

I think we should remember that in spite of all the scientific advances and the great improvements in our material welfare the family remains as the focal point of our existence. There is overwhelming evidence that those who cannot experience full and happy family life for some reason or another are deprived of a great stabilizing influence in their lives.

At Christmas we are also reminded that it is the time of peace on earth and good will towards men. Yet we are all only too well aware of the tragic fighting, hatred and ill will in so many parts of the world.

Because of this, cynics may shrug off the Christmas message as a waste of time. But that is only the gloomy side of the picture: there are also brighter and more hopeful signs. The great churches of the world are coming to understand each other better and to recognize that without their inspiration and great ideals mankind will be smothered by its own material wealth. We must have dreams and ambitions for peace and good will and they must be proclaimed.

Perhaps the most practical demonstration of good will towards men is to be found in the growing practice among young people to give some form of voluntary service to others. In Britain and throughout the world they are coming forward to help old people or to serve in every kind of capacity where they may be needed at home and overseas.

A new army is on the march which holds out the brightest hopes for all mankind. It serves in international work-camps, in areas hit by natural disasters or emergencies, and in helping the poor, the backward or the hungry.

Peace on earth – we may not have it at the moment, we may never have it completely, but we will certainly achieve nothing unless we go on trying to remove the causes of conflict between peoples and nations.

Good will towards men is not a hollow phrase. Good will exists and when there is an opportunity to show it in practical form we know what wonderful things it can achieve. To deny this Christmas message is to admit defeat and to give up hope.

It is a rejection of everything that makes life worth living, and, what is far worse, it offers nothing in its place. In fact, it is just because there are so many conflicts in the world today that we should reaffirm our hopes and beliefs in a more peaceful and a more friendly world in the future. This is just the moment to remind ourselves that we can all find some practical way to serve others and help to create a better understanding between people.

To each one of you I wish a very happy Christmas and if throughout the Commonwealth we can all make a sustained effort perhaps Christmas next year will be a much happier one for many more people.

It is difficult to realise that it was less than 50 years ago that women in Britain were first given the vote, but Parliament was first asked to grant this 100 years ago.

Yet, in spite of these disabilities, it has been women who have breathed gentleness and care into the harsh progress of mankind.

The struggles against inhuman prejudice, against squalor, ignorance, and disease, have always owed a great deal to the determination and tenacity of women.

The devotion of nuns and nurses, the care of mothers and wives, the services of teachers, and the conviction of reformers are the real and enduring presents which women have always given.

In the modern world the opportunities for women to give something of value to the human family are greater than ever, because, through their own efforts, they are now beginning to play their full part in public life.

We know so much more about what can be achieved: we know that the tyranny of ignorance can be broken: we know the rules of health and how to protect children from disease.

We know all these things are important in our own homes, but it needs a very active concern by women everywhere if this knowledge is to be used where it is most needed. I am glad that in all countries of the Commonwealth women are more and more able to use it.

I am sure the custom of giving presents at Christmas will never die out, but I hope it will never overshadow the far more important presents we can give for the benefit of the future of the world.

People of goodwill everywhere are working to build a world that will be a happier and more peaceful place in which to live. Let our prayers be for a personal strength and conviction to play our own small part to bring that day nearer.

God be with you, and a very happy Christmas to you all.

E ver since the first Christmas, when the Three Wise Men brought their presents, Christians all over the world have kept up this kindly custom.

Even if the presents we give each other at Christmas-time may only be intended to give momentary pleasure, they do also reflect one all-important lesson.

Society cannot hope for a just and peaceful civilisation unless each individual feels the need to be concerned about his fellows.

All the great works of charity and all humanitarian legislation have always been inspired by a flame of compassion which has burnt brightly in the hearts of men and women.

Mankind has many blemishes, but deep down in every human soul there is a store of goodwill waiting to be called upon.

This year I should like to speak especially to women. In many countries custom has decreed that women should play a minor part in public affairs.

Top left:
Queen Elizabeth II smiling at a Colonel of the 1st Battalion of the Irish Guards during a presentation of colours ceremony at Buckingham Palace, London.

Below:
Queen Elizabeth II smiles after presenting England captain Bobby Moore with the Jules Rimet trophy, following England's 4 – 2 victory over West Germany in the World Cup Final at Wembley Stadium, London.

1966

Left:
Mini skirts caused a furore when they first hit the fashion scene, but before long it was not only the young and beautiful who were showing a few inches of thigh. And hemlines rose a little with each passing year.

Right:
England team members carry their captain Bobby Moore shoulder high as he brandishes the World Cup.

World Events of 1966

Floods in north Italy ruin thousands of art treasures in Florence.
In London, Myra Hindley and Ian Brady go on trial at the Old Bailey for the "Moors Murders".
Mao Tse-tung proclaims a Cultural Revolution in China.
Indira Gandhi becomes Prime Minister of India.
Britain is replaced by Japan as Australia's best trade customer.
In America, the first black senator, Edward W. Brooke, is elected.
Random roadside breathalysers are introduced in Britain.
Supermarkets are becoming popular throughout Europe and the Far East.
The Labour government declares a State of Emergency because of a seamen's strike.
Barcelona police beat up 100 priests protesting at police brutality.
83-year-old Eamon de Valera is re-elected President of Ireland.
Race riots flare up in the US.

Sporting Life

Boxer Cassius Clay beats Henry Cooper to retain the world heavyweight championship.
England footballers beat Germany to win the World Cup 4 – 2.
In tennis, Australia defeats India in the Davis Cup.
Billie-Jean King wins the women's singles title at Wimbledon.
In horse racing, the Cheltenham Gold Cup is won by Arkle for the third year running.

The Arts

The Mamas and the Papas introduce soft rock.
Hit songs are 'Eleanor Rigby' and 'Strangers in the Night'.
Frank Sinatra and Mia Farrow marry.
The Beatles play their last live concert.
Elizabeth Taylor stars in 'Who's Afraid of Virgina Woolf?'
In London, the West End's longest running musical 'Oliver!' ends its run of six years, three months.

1967

World Events of 1967

In Cape Town, the world's first human heart transplant is successfully carried out.

British yachtsman Francis Chichester completes a solo round the world voyage.

Israel wages a Six-Day War against the Arab states.

The microwave oven is introduced in the US.

President Lyndon Johnson visits the US troops in Vietnam.

Britain's largest new town will occupy 22,000 acres of Buckinghamshire and be called "Milton Keynes".

In Britain, ITV starts broadcasting "News At Ten", a daily half-hour news programme.

The British model Twiggy hits the fashion world.

Donald Campbell dies attempting to break the world water speed record.

In Britain's biggest ever bullion raid, £700,000 in gold bars is stolen from a security van.

In Nigeria, government troops invade Biafra and Europeans flee.

In Britain, the £8 million Dartford Tunnel under the Thames opens.

Che Guevara, Argentinian revolutionary, is shot dead.

Sporting Life

In England 100 – 1 outsider Foinavov wins this year's Grand National.

Heavyweight boxer Muhammad Ali (formely Cassius Clay) is indicted for refusing to fight in Vietnam.

In cricket, South Africa defeats Australia 3 tests to 1 in South Africa.

In Monaco, a Mini Cooper wins the Monte Carlo rally.

In baseball, St Louis Cardinals beat the Boston Red Sox to win the World Series.

The Arts

Dustin Hoffman stars in 'The Graduate'.

Elizabeth Taylor wins an Oscar for 'Who's Afraid of Virginia Woolf?'

'A Man For All Seasons' wins six Oscars.

Elvis Presley marries Priscilla Beaulieu.

Hit songs are 'Release Me' and 'All You Need is Love'.

The Beatles release the 'Sergeant Pepper's' album.

Below left:
After the Six Day Arab-Israeli war, the West Bank was occupied by Israel.

Below:
The Russian agent Kim Philby fled to the Soviet Union in 1963 where he eventually became a senior officer in the KGB. In 1967 he gave his first interview to British journalists.

Right:
Queen Elizabeth II inspects the Royal Green Jackets Regiment at Winchester.

Prince Philip and I went to Ottawa for the centenary celebrations and it was a most moving occasion. Canada has every reason to feel proud of her achievements in the last 100 years. Confederation as a formal act could have achieved little by itself. Only the determined will of a great variety of individuals and groups to cooperate for the greater national interest could have breathed life into the creation of the fathers of confederation.

The future of Canada as a great and prosperous country depends just as much on the will of the present generation to work together.

The lasting impression which I took away with me from Canada's centennial and Expo '67 is the degree of unity in outlook among the diverse nations, creeds and races of the world.

The Commonwealth is a system which is in a constant process of change and development. This was brought home to me vividly when I revisited Malta only a month ago. When I first went to the islands, they were a colony and my husband was serving with the Mediterranean Fleet. Today Malta is independent, with the Crown occupying the same position as it does in the other self-governing countries of which I am Queen. This is the opening of a new and challenging chapter for the people of Malta, and they are entering it with determination and enthusiasm.

Great national events can stir the imagination, but so can individual actions. Few people can have attracted so much universal attention as Sir Francis Chichester during his epic journey in 'Gipsy Moth'. I am sure that the reason his great feat of seamanship so warmed our hearts was that we recognized in his enterprise and courage the very qualities which have played such a large part in British history, and which we in these islands need just as much today and for the future.

Let there be no doubt that Britain is faced with formidable problems, but let there also be no doubt she will overcome them. Determined and well directed effort from a people who for centuries have given ample evidence of their resources of character and initiative must bring its reward.

I am glad to say that contact at all levels between Commonwealth countries continues to grow, and I have been delighted to welcome Commonwealth Prime Ministers and leaders in various walks of life.

Among the people who attract the greatest attention are visiting sportsmen and athletes. Cricket teams from India and Pakistan braved the vagaries of the English summer, and the redoubtable All-Blacks from New Zealand have made a solid impact on British Rugby footballers. Kenya sent us her great runner Keino. I hope many more sportsmen from Africa will take part in competitions and will establish new contacts between Africa and the rest of the world.

My two elder children came back from the Commonwealth Games in Jamaica enchanted with the adventure, the kindness of the people, and the opportunity to meet so many athletes from every part of the Commonwealth. For my son this came at the end of a period in Australia which he would not have missed for anything and where the exciting challenges and opportunities deeply impressed him.

In October this year, I took my son and daughter with me to the opening of Parliament at Westminster. The opening of Parliament is not just a ritual. It should remind us that Parliament symbolizes the nation.

You may have heard it very often, but in the end no matter what scientific progress we make, the message will count for nothing unless we can achieve real peace and encourage genuine good will between individual people and the nations of the world.

Every Christmas I am sustained and encouraged by the happiness and sense of unity which comes from seeing all the members of my family together. I hope and pray that, with God's help, this Christmas spirit of family unity will spread and grow among our Commonwealth family of nations.

Christmas is a Christian festival which celebrates the birth of the Prince of Peace. At times it is almost hidden by the merry-making and tinsel, but the essential message of Christmas is still that we all belong to the great brotherhood of man.

This idea is not limited to the Christian faith. Philosophers and prophets have concluded that peace is better than war, love is better than hate and that mankind can only find progress in friendship and co-operation.

Many ideas are being questioned today, but these great truths will continue to shine out as the light of hope in the darkness of intolerance and inhumanity.

The words "the brotherhood of man" have a splendid ring about them, but the idea may seem too remote to have any practical meaning in this hard and bustling age. Indeed it means nothing at all unless the brotherhood, starting with individuals, can reconcile rival communities, conflicting religions, differing races and the divided and prejudiced nations of the world.

If we truly believe that the brotherhood of man has a value for the world's future, then we should seek to support those international organisations which foster understanding between people and between nations.

The British people together have achieved great things in the past and have overcome many dangers, but we cannot make further progress if we resurrect ancient squabbles.

The nations belonging to the Commonwealth have in their hands a well-tried framework for mutual help and co-operation. It would be short-sighted to waste this modest step towards brotherhood because we are too busy with the dissensions of the moment.

Every individual and every nation have problems, so there is all the more reason for us to do our utmost to show our concern for others.

Rich or poor, we all depend upon the work and skill of individual men and women, particularly those in industry and production who are the creators of wealth and prosperity. We depend on new knowledge, invention and innovation, practical improvements and developments, all of which offer us a better life.

Yet we should not be obsessed by material problems. We must also be sure that we remain spiritually alive. Everything we do now is helping to shape the world in which our children are going to live. Our young people need all the help and opportunities we can give them to prepare them for the responsibilities which they will soon have to carry.

Today I have spoken of "the brotherhood of man" and the hope it holds out for the world. This should not remain a vague thought nor an abstract idea. Each of us can put it into practice by treating one another with kindness and consideration at all times and in spite of every kind of provocation.

Christmas is the festival of peace. It is God's will that it should be our constant endeavour to establish "peace on earth, good will towards men".

I hope you all have a very happy Christmas and every good fortune in the new year.

1968

World Events of 1968

Richard Nixon is elected President of the United States.

In Egypt, the Aswan Dam is completed.

The Civil rights leader Dr Martin Luther King is assassinated in Memphis.

Russia invades Czechoslovakia.

Anti-Vietnam demonstrations take place in London.

French students revolt in Paris.

Robert Kennedy is shot dead.

Anti-government protests break out in Warsaw.

Abortion is legalised in Britain.

There is a wave of student riots throughout Europe following the shooting of left-wing student leader Rudi Dutschke.

The first decimal coins come into circulation in the UK – 5 New Pence and 10 New Pence.

President Charles de Gaulle has a landslide victory in France's general election.

The epidural technique, a new method of relieving pain in child birth, is used for the first time.

In London, the Family Law Reform Bill is published, aiming to lower the age of adulthood from 21 to 18.

Sporting Life

Rod Laver beats fellow Australian Tony Roche to win Wimbledon.

The Olympic Games are held in Mexico City.

In cricket, Australia defeats India 4 tests to nil.

English football team Manchester United win the European Cup.

Tony Jacklin is the first English golfer to win a major US golf tournament for more than 20 years.

The Arts

Hit songs are 'Hey Jude', 'Wonderful World' and 'Those Were the Days'.

The musical 'Hair' opens in London.

John Updike's novel 'Couples' is published.

American novelist John Steinbeck dies.

The film '2001: A Space Odyssey' is released.

Below:
Attempts to reform the communist system in Czechoslovakia led to an invasion by the USSR and their allies who feared that reform would spread to their countries.

1969

1969

Top right:
"One small step for man; one giant leap for mankind." Apollo 11 made the first manned lunar landing on July 20 1969. Millions watched on TV as Eagle, the lunar excursion module, approached the moon's surface. Neil Armstrong was the first man to walk on the moon, followed by Edwin "Buzz" Aldrin. Michael Collins piloted the command module.

Bottom right:
British troops were sent into Northern Ireland to deal with civil unrest and try to establish peace between Catholics demonstrating for basic rights and extremist Protestant mobs. The military presence continued until the Peace Agreement of 1998.

World Events of 1969

War breaks out between El Salvador and Honduras after a football match.
Israel elects its first woman premier, Golda Meir.
Inflation is a worldwide problem.
The Open University begins its courses in the UK.
The first man, Neil Armstrong, lands on the moon.
Yasser Arafat is appointed the new leader of the PLO.
The Woodstock Festival in the US is attended by some 400,000 people.
Britain is admitted into the EEC.
British troops move into Belfast.
The Kray twins are jailed for 30 years.
At the age of 22, Bernadette Devlin becomes the youngest ever British MP.
Colonel Gaddafi becomes leader of Libya.
In New York, two university campuses are closed because of student rioting.
First colour transmissions in Britain are made by the ITV.

Sporting Life

Manchester City beat Leicester City to win the English FA Cup Final.
Golfer Tony Jacklin wins the British Open.
The US tennis team retains the Davis Cup, beating the Rumanians.
Brazilian football star Pele scores his 1000th goal.
In cricket, Australia defeats the West Indies 3 tests to 1.

The Arts

Frank Sinatra releases 'My Way'.
Beatles star Paul McCartney marries Linda Eastman.
Mario Puzo's book 'The Godfather' is published.
The Rolling Stones play at Madison Gardens, US.

Hit songs are 'My Way' and 'Gentle on My Mind'.
Rolling Stones member Brian Jones drowns at the age of 25.

Dennis Hopper stars in the film 'Easy Rider'.
French novelist Samuel Beckett is awarded the Nobel Prize for Literature.

I have received a great number of kind letters and messages of regard and concern about this year's break with the usual broadcast at Christmas and I want you all to know that my good wishes are no less warm and personal because they come to you in a different form.

In a short time the 1960s will be over but not out of our memories. Historians will record them as the decade in which men first reached out beyond our own planet and set foot on the moon, but each one of us will have our own special triumphs or tragedies to look back on.

My own thoughts are with my older children who are entering the service of the people of this country and the Commonwealth. It is a great satisfaction and comfort to me and my husband to know that they have won a place in your affections.

We are all looking forward to our visit to Australia and New Zealand for the Cook bicentenary celebrations, and also to Fiji and Tonga. Later next year we hope to see something of the fascinating development of northern Canada.

It is only natural that we should all be dazzled and impressed by the triumphs of technology, but Christmas is a festival of the spirit.

At this time our concern is particularly for the lonely, the sick and the elderly. I hope they will all feel the warmth and comfort of companionship and that all of you will enjoy a very happy Christmas with your families and friends.

God bless you all.

Every year we are reminded that Christmas is a family festival; a time for reunion and a meeting point for the generations.

This year I am thinking of rather a special family – a family of nations – as I recall fascinating journeys literally to opposite ends of the world.

During the course of these visits we met and talked with a great number of people in every sort of occupation, and living in every kind of community and climate. Yet in all this diversity they had one thing in common; they were all members of the Commonwealth family.

Early this year we went to Fiji, Tonga, New Zealand and Australia in 'Britannia'. We were following the path taken in 1770 by that great English discoverer, Captain Cook.

A little later in the year we were in Canada. Still in the Commonwealth, visiting the North-West Territories and Manitoba for their centenaries.

Among people who are so essentially New Zealanders, Canadians or Australians, it struck me again that so many of them still have affectionate and personal links with the British Isles.

Wherever I went among people living in the busy industrial towns or on the stations and farms of the far outback, I met newcomers who reminded me that these links between our countries are renewed every year.

In Canada, we met some of the older inhabitants – Indians – people whose ancestors were there for generations before the Europeans came. And further north still live the Esquimaux, some of the most interesting people that we met during our travels this year. They too belong to the Commonwealth family, this remarkable collection of friendly people of so many races.

Later in the year, representatives from 42 different parts of the world gathered to attend the Commonwealth Games. There are many unpublicised meetings, but it is not often that the Commonwealth is able to get together for a great public ceremony. On this occasion it was sport that brought them to Scotland, and they came to compete and to enjoy themselves.

We entertained them all in the garden of our home in Edinburgh, and I was very conscious that each of the athletes I met represented a country as different and interesting as those I had been able to visit during the year.

Never before has there been a group of independent nations linked in this way by their common history and continuing affection.

Too often we hear about the Commonwealth only when there is bad news about one of its members, or when its usefulness or its very existence is questioned. Britain and other members responded generously after the terrible disaster in East Pakistan, but the fellowship of the Commonwealth does not exist only at such unhappy times.

Many of us here in Britain have relatives living in other Commonwealth countries, and there are many who were born overseas living here. Because it is Christmas we are probably thinking of them now. It is these personal contacts which mean so much.

The strength of the Commonwealth lies in its history and the way people feel about it. All those years through which we have lived together have given us an exchange of people and ideas which ensures that there is a continuing concern for each other.

That, very simply, is the message of Christmas – learning to be concerned about one another; to treat your neighbour as you would like him to treat you, and to care about the future of all life on earth. These matters of the spirit are more important and more lasting than simple material development. It is a hard lesson, but I like to think that we in the Commonwealth have perhaps begun to understand it.

I wish you a merry Christmas. God bless you all.

Right:
From the left, British Prime Minister Edward Heath, Queen Elizabeth II of Great Britain, Richard Nixon, President of the United States of America at Chequers.

World Events of 1970

Edward Heath becomes British Prime Minister.
The Beatles officially split.
The "Hong Kong" flu kills 2,850 people in Britain in one week.
US troops are sent to Cambodia.
Violence erupts at the Suez Canal.
Arab terrorists hijack five aeroplanes and explode three.
Charles de Gaulle dies in France.
In Britain, the age of voting is reduced from 21 to 18.
In Ceylon, Mrs Bandaranaike is re-elected Prime Minister.
Cambodia is declared a republic.

Sporting Life

South Africa is banned from the 1972 Olympics.
Australia loses the Americas Cup 4 to 1.
British golfer Tony Jacklin wins the US Open.
Brazil wins football's World Cup.

The Arts

John Wayne wins an Oscar for 'True Grit'.
Janis Joplin dies.
The film M*A*S*H wins first prize at the Cannes Film Festival.
Hit songs are 'Yellow River', 'The Wonder of You' and 'In the Summertime'.
Guitarist Jimi Hendrix dies at the age of 28.
Bernice Rubens wins the Booker Prize for her novel 'The Elected Member'.

Right:
The genius of composer and rock guitarist Jimi Hendrix was cut short by his tragic death on September 18 1970. His unique sound has inspired many of today's great rock musicians.

1971

World Events of 1971

Britain converts to decimal currency.
Riots break out in Ulster, Northern Ireland.
Two American astronauts go for a drive on the moon.
The bombing of North Vietnam continues.
Bangladesh becomes independent.
China joins the UN, against the protests of US and Taiwan.
Idi Amin becomes dictator in Uganda.
In the UK, the first divorce is granted under the Divorce Act.
On the French Riviera, hundreds of women are ordered to put their bikini tops back on.
Britain expels 90 Russians for spying.
Mount Etna erupts.

Sporting Life

British boxer Henry Cooper retires from the ring.
The Australian tennis player Evonne Goolagong wins Wimbledon.
British golfers win the Walker Cup for the first time since 1938.

The Arts

Glenda Jackson stars in 'Women in Love'.
Sylvia Plath's novel 'The Bell Jar' is published posthumously.
Hit songs are 'Chirpy, Chirpy, Cheep, Cheep' and 'Maggie May'.
Anthony Burgess' novel 'A Clockwork Orange' is made into a film.
'Love Story' by Eric Segal is published.

Right:
The Lunar *Rover*, the first manned surface vehicle was transported to the moon by Apollo 15. Many experiments were carried out on the moon's surface, and 77 kg of soil and rocks were brought back to earth to be analysed.

Christmas is the time for families and for children, and it is also a time when we realize that another year is coming to an end. As the familiar pattern of Christmas and the new year repeats itself, we may sometimes forget how much the world about us has been changing.

It was 39 years ago that my grandfather, King George V, gave the first of his Christmas broadcasts. He spoke about a future which is now the past. Today it is our turn to think about the future.

Many of you who are listening are able, like me, to enjoy this Christmas with your families, and your children can enjoy the day as all children should. But tragically, there are many millions of others for whom this cannot be the same. Our thoughts and prayers should be for them.

Our children will be living in a world which our work and deeds have shaped for them. We cannot possibly tell what changes the next 40 years will bring. We do know that we are passing on to our children the power to change their whole environment. But we also leave them with a set of values which they take from our lives and from our example. The decisions they take and the sort of world they pass on to their children could be just as much affected by those values as by all the technological wonders of this age.

If we can show this by our lives and by our example, then our contribution as parents will be just as important as any made by scientists and engineers. Perhaps we can then look for the real peace on earth, and the powers which men have harnessed will be used for the benefit of our fellow men.

Above: Emperor Hirohito of Japan (1901 – 1989) with Queen Elizabeth II, Empress Nagako, Prince Charles and Princess Margaret Rose (far right). The Emperor is wearing the insignia of the Order of the Garter.

One of the great Christian ideals is a happy and lasting marriage between man and wife, but no marriage can hope to succeed without a deliberate effort to be tolerant and understanding. This doesn't come easily to communities or nations. We know only too well that a selfish insistence upon our rights and on our own point of view leads to disaster.

We all ought to know by now that a civilised and peaceful existence is only possible when people make the effort to understand each other. Looking at the world, one might be forgiven for believing that many people have never heard of this simple idea.

Every day there are reports of violence, lawlessness and the disregard for human life. Most of this is excused on purely selfish grounds. I know there are millions of kindly people throughout the world who are saddened with me for all those who suffer from these outrages.

But there is a light in this tragic situation. The people are steadfastly carrying on their ordinary business in their factories and places of work. Voluntary workers, both in and out of uniform, have struggled to keep humanity and commonsense alive.

The social services have done their job magnificently. The forces of law and order continue their thankless task with the utmost fortitude in the face of appalling provocation. We admire them greatly for their patience and restraint.

I ask you all to join me in praying that the hearts and minds of everyone in that troubled province may be touched with the spirit of Christmas and the message of brotherhood, peace and good will. May tolerance and understanding release the people from terror and put gladness in the place of fear.

In this unique organisation we are fortunate in having endless opportunities for cooperation. Through its informal structure we have created a web of relationships between peoples of many races and creeds ... and now between a great number of sovereign independent states.

Britain is about to join her neighbours in the European Community and you may well ask how this will affect the Commonwealth. The new links with Europe will not replace those with the Commonwealth. They cannot alter our historical and personal attachments with kinsmen and friends overseas. Old friends will not be lost; Britain will take her Commonwealth links into Europe with her.

Britain and these other European countries see in the Community a new opportunity for the future. They believe that the things they have in common are more important than the things which divide them, and that if they work together not only they but the whole world will benefit.

We are trying to create a wider family of nations and it is particularly at Christmas that this family should feel closest together. Christmas is above all a time of new life. A time to look hopefully ahead to a future when the problems which face the world today will be seen in their true perspective.

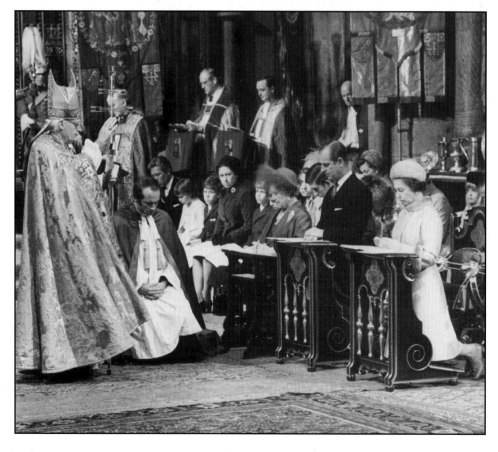

Right:
Archbishiop of Canterbury Dr Arthur Ramsey blesses Queen Elizabeth II and Prince Philip, the Duke of Edingburgh, during a Service of Thanksgiving at Westminster Abbey, London, to celebrate their Silver Wedding Anniversary.

1972

World Events of 1972

The 'Queen Elizabeth' liner is destroyed by fire in Hong Kong.

Arab terrorists massacre 11 Israeli athletes at the Munich Olympics.

Miners strike in Britain.

Violence increases in Northern Ireland, leading to the "Bloody Sunday" killings in Ulster.

'Apollo 17' makes its longest and final visit to the moon.

10,000 people die in an earthquake in Nicaragua.

West Germany signs non-aggression pacts with the Soviet Union and Poland.

Britain signs the EEC treaty.

Richard Nixon is re-elected President of the US.

Richard Nixon makes a historic visit to China – the first ever by a US President.

Later he makes a visit to Moscow, again scoring another first.

Police arrest five men for breaking into the Democratic Party Headquaters in the Watergate office complex in Washington DC. The ensuing Watergate scandal was to run for years.

US ground troops finally withdraw from Vietnam, though the war is not yet fully over.

Sporting Life

Stan Smith wins Wimbledon's men's singles final.

American swimmer Mark Spitz wins a record seven gold medals in the Olympics.

Russian gymnast Olga Korbut wins three gold medals at the Olympics.

Arab terrorists strike at the Israeli team participating in the Munich Olympics, leaving 11 dead and many wounded.

Bobby Fischer becomes the first American to win the world championship by beating the USSR's Boris Spassky.

The Arts

Liza Minnelli stars in 'Cabaret'.

King Tutankhamun's treasures are exhibited in Britain.

Hit songs are 'Amazing Grace' and 'Puppy Love'.

Marlon Brando stars in the film 'The Godfather'.

Alfred Hitchcock directs the film 'Frenzy'.

Richard Adams' 'Watership Down' is published.

In London, John Betjeman is appointed Poet Laureate.

Dirty Harry turns journey-man actor Clint Eastwood into a film icon and his "feel lucky, punk?" line into a popular catchphrase.

Barbara Streisand was the years most popular female star for her roles in 'Whats Up Doc?' and 'Up the Sandbox'.

Jane Fonda received far more press coverage, but for her role in protest at the Vietnam War, as she visited Hanoi.

Richard Bach's 'Jonathan Livingston Seagull', an existential tale about an individualistic seagull, tops the best-seller lists.

Above:
11 Israeli athletes were massacred by Palestinian terrorists in Munich.

Left:
In October John Betjeman, poet and architectural critic was appointed British Poet Laureate. He succeeded Cecil Day Lewis, who died in May.

1973

Right:
Right:
On October 6th, Israel was invaded by Egypt and Syria on the religious holiday of the Day of Atonement (Yom Kippur). These first assaults were soon strengthened by forces from Iraq, Morocco, Saudi Arabia and Jordan.However, despite the substantial forces ranged against her, Israel retaliated and advanced into Egypt and Syria.

Below:
Pedal-power in Italy during the fuel crisis.

World Events of 1973

Princess Anne and Captain Mark Phillips marry at Westminster Abbey.
Crown Prince Carl Gustaf becomes King of Sweden.
There is a ceasefire in Vietnam.
The Watergate scandal breaks in Washington.
Yom Kippur war erupts between Israel and Egypt.
In Athens, Greece is declared a Republic.
John Paul Getty III is kidnapped.
The World Trade Center is completed in New York.
Britain, Denmark and Ireland join the EEC.
VAT is introduced in the UK.
East and West Germany establish diplomatic relations.
Three manned Skylab stations are successfully launched over a three-month period.
From May to November the live broadcasts of the Watergate trial transfix America.

Sporting Life

Star tennis players boycott Wimbledon.
Ajax Amsterdam win football's European Cup for the third year running.
The Grand National is won in a record time of nine minutes 1.9 seconds by 'Red Rum'.
George Foreman beats Joe Frazier for the World Heavyweight boxing title.
OJ Simpson sets an unbeaten seasonal record for rushing yardage in American Football, becomes a household name with movie roles and product endorsements.

The Arts

Artist Pablo Picasso dies at the age of 91.
The film 'Jesus Christ Superstar' is released.
Robert Redford and Paul Newman star in 'The Sting'.
Erica Jong's book 'Fear of Flying' is published.

Hit songs are 'Tie a Yellow Ribbon' and 'Blockbuster'.
'The Exorcist' is released.
'Kojak' TV series makes Telly Savalas, the bald, lolly-pop sucking New York cop a household name.
Glenda Jackson receives an Oscar for her role in 'A Touch of Class'.
Bruce Lee, star of countless Kung Fu films dies of a brain edema, having just made it big in the US.
Marlon Brando and Maria Schneider star in Bernardo Bertolucci's 'Last Tango in Paris'.

Above: April saw the death of Spanish artist Pablo Picasso (1881 – 1973). He was 91.

It is now 21 years since I first broadcast a Christmas Message to the Commonwealth.

Then our two elder children were only four and two. Now our daughter joins us for Christmas with her husband and we are celebrating the festival this year with the memories of their wedding very much in our minds.

We are constantly being told that we live in a changing world and that we need to adapt to changing conditions. But this is only part of the truth and I am sure that all parents seeing their children getting married are reminded of the continuity of human life.

That is why, I think, that at weddings all friends and relations, and even complete strangers, can stop worrying for a moment, and share in the happiness of the couple who are getting married.

I am glad that my daughter's wedding gave such pleasure to so many people, just at a time when the world was facing very serious problems.

People all over the world watched the wedding on television, but there were still many in London on the day, and their warmth and enthusiasm ensured it was an occasion my family will never forget.

Earlier this year, I went to Canada for a different sort of family occasion. This was the meeting of Commonwealth Heads of Government and here, I was reminded of the importance of human relationships in world affairs, and how membership of the Commonwealth has a subtle influence on the relationships between its leaders.

I was impressed by the spirit which brought together so many leaders from such different countries and enabled them to discuss constructively matters which concern us all as friends.

Those of you who are surrounded by friends – or, of course, who are members of a happy family – know this makes life much easier. Everything – the good and the bad – can be shared but it is too easy for us to forget those who are not so fortunate.

However, there are many people of all ages who go out to help the old and the lonely, the sick and the handicapped. I am sure that, in so doing, they find the real happiness that comes from serving and thinking of others.

I believe that Christmas should remind us that the qualities of the human spirit are more important than material gain. Christ taught love and charity and that we should show humanity and compassion at all times and in all situations.

A lack of humanity and compassion can be very destructive – how easily this causes divisions within nations and between nations. We should remember instead how much we have in common and resolve to give expression to the best of our human qualities, not only at Christmas, but right through the year.

In this Christmas spirit let us greet all our fellow men and join together in this festival of tolerance and companionship.

I wish you all a very happy Christmas.

Left:
Princess Anne the Princess Royal and Captain Mark Phillips with members of their immediate and extended family at Buckingham Palace after their wedding.

1974

World Events of 1974

Britain's first McDonald's restaurant opens in London.

Cyclone Fifi in Honduras kills 10,000 people.

President Nixon is the first US President to resign from power, and is succeeded by Gerald Ford.

Heiress Patty Hearst is kidnapped in California.

French President Georges Pompidou dies and is succeeded by Giscard d'Estaing.

Lord Lucan is sought in Britain and Europe for the murder of his nanny, and an attack on his estranged wife.

Prince Juan Carlos takes over from Franco in Spain.

Turkey invades Cyprus.

In Australia, a cyclone hits Darwin.

Sporting Life

West Germany win football's World Cup.

Tennis couple Jimmy Connors and Chris Evert both win their respective Wimbledon singles titles.

The Arts

Ballet dancer Mikhail Baryshnikov defects from Russia.

Hit songs are 'Seasons in the Sun' and 'The Way We Were'.

Robert Redford stars in 'The Great Gatsby'.

John Le Carre's book 'Tinker, Tailor, Soldier, Spy' is published.

Abba win the Eurovision Song Contest with 'Waterloo'.

Jack Nicholson stars in 'Chinatown'.

Right:
Richard Nixon resigned as President of the United States when it was revealed that he was implicated in the Watergate scandal, in which White House officials had obstructed investigations into a burglary at the Democratic Party headquarters.

Right:
Queen Elizabeth II giving the royal salute during a Trooping of the Colour ceremony at Horse Guards' Parade, London.

There can be few people in any country of the Commonwealth who are not anxious about what is happening in their own countries or in the rest of the world at this time.

We have never been short of problems, but in the last year everything seems to have happened at once. There have been floods and drought and famine: there have been outbreaks of senseless violence. And on top of it all the cost of living continues to rise – everywhere.

Here in Britain, from where so many people of the Commonwealth came, we hear a great deal about our troubles, about discord and dissension and about the uncertainty of our future.

Perhaps we make too much of what is wrong and too little of what is right. The trouble with gloom is that it feeds upon itself and depression causes more depression.

There are indeed real dangers and there are real fears and we will never overcome them if we turn against each other with angry accusations.

We may hold different points of view but it is in times of stress and difficulty that we most need to remember that we have much more in common than there is dividing us. We have the lessons of history to show that the British people have survived many a desperate situation when they acted together.

People in a crowd may seem oblivious of each other. Yet if you look at your neighbours you will see other people with worries and difficulties probably greater than your own. It is time to recognise that in the end we all depend upon each other and that we are therefore responsible for each other.

Fortunately over the centuries we have devised a way of sharing this responsibility, a uniquely effective system for bringing progress out of conflict.

We have developed Parliamentary Government by which the rights and freedom of the people are maintained.

It allows change to take place temperately and without violence. And when time demands, it can reflect and give a voice to the determination and resolve of the Nation.

This system, this product of British genius, has been successfully exported to the world-wide Commonwealth.

This year I have opened Parliament four times: in New Zealand, in Australia, and twice the Mother of Parliaments in Westminster. I suspect this may be a record, but what impressed me was that the system itself flourishes thousands of miles away and this alone should give us confidence.

You may be asking what can we do personally to make things better?

I believe the Christmas message provides the best clue. Goodwill is better than resentment, tolerance is better than revenge, compassion is better than anger, above all a lively concern for the interests of others as well as our own. In times of doubt and anxiety the attitudes people show in their daily lives, in their homes, and in their work, are of supreme importance.

It is by acting in this spirit that every man, woman and child can help and "make a difference".

In Britain I am sure it could make all the difference. We are an inventive and tenacious people and the comradeship of adversity brings out the best in us. And we have great resources, not just those of character but in our industry and trade, in our farms and in the seas around our shores.

My message today is one of encouragement and hope.

Christmas on this side of the equator comes at the darkest time of year: but we can look forward hopefully to lengthening days and the returning sun.

The first Christmas came at a time that was dark and threatening, but from it came the light of the world.

I wish you all a happy Christmas.

Every year I have this special opportunity of wishing you a happy Christmas. I like to think I am speaking to each child who can hear me, each woman, every man in every country of the Commonwealth.

Christmas is a festival which brings us together in small groups, a family group if we are lucky. Today we are not just nameless people in a crowd. We meet as friends who are glad to be together and who care about each other's happiness.

Nowadays this is a precious experience. So much of the time we feel that our lives are dominated by great impersonal forces beyond our control; the scale of things and organisations seems to get bigger and more inhuman. We are horrified by brutal and senseless violence and, above all, the whole fabric of our lives is threatened by inflation, the frightening sickness of the world today.

Then Christmas comes, and once again we are reminded that people matter and it is our relationship with one another that is most important.

For most of us – I wish it could be for everyone – this is a holiday, and I think it is worth reminding ourselves why. We are celebrating a birthday – the birthday of a child born nearly 2000 years ago, who grew up and lived for only about 30 years.

That one person, by his example and by his revelation of the good which is in us all, has made an enormous difference to the lives of people who have come to understand his teaching. His simple message of love has been turning the world upside down ever since.

He showed that what people are and what they do does matter and does make all the difference.

He commanded us to love our neighbours as we love ourselves, but what exactly is meant by "loving ourselves"? I believe it means trying to make the most of the abilities we have been given. It means caring for our talents. It is a matter of making the best of ourselves, not just doing the best for ourselves.

We are all different, but each of us has his own best to offer. The responsibility for the way we live life, with all its challenges, sadness and joy, is ours alone. If we do this well, it will also be good for our neighbours.

If you throw a stone into a pool, the ripples go on spreading outwards. A big stone can cause waves, but even the smallest pebble changes the whole pattern of the water. Our daily actions are like those ripples, each one makes a difference, even the smallest.

It does matter therefore what each individual does each day. Kindness, sympathy, resolution and courteous behaviour are infectious.

Acts of courage and self-sacrifice, like those of the people who refuse to be terrorised by kidnappers or hijackers or who defuse bombs, are an inspiration to others.

And the combined effect can be enormous. If enough grains of sand are dropped into one side of a pair of scales they will, in the end, tip it against a lump of lead.

We may feel powerless alone, but the joint efforts of individuals can defeat the evils of our time. Together they can create a stable, free and considerate society. Like those grains of sand, they can tip the balance; so take heart from the Christmas message and be happy.

God bless you all

Left:
Queen Elizabeth II, together with Peter Lawrence, during a visit to the Silverwood Colliery in Rotherham.

Below:
Queen Elizabeth II at a market stall during a royal tour of Hong Kong.

1975

World Events of 1975

The Suez Canal re-opens after eight years.

The monarchy returns to Spain with Juan Carlos becoming King.

A terracotta army of 6,000 life-sized soldiers dating from the 3rd century BC is discovered in China.

The last US troops leave Saigon.

In Hawaii, Mauna Loa volcano erupts.

The Channel Tunnel is abandoned by the British Government.

The Khmer Rouge overrun Cambodia.

Over 6.5 million elm trees are killed by Dutch elm disease in England.

Margaret Thatcher becomes the first woman leader of a British political party.

Sporting Life

Czechoslovakian tennis player Martina Navratilova defects to the US.

The West Indies win cricket's first World Cup.

At 23, Anatoly Karpov becomes the world's youngest chess champion.

Arthur Ashe is the first black men's singles champion at Wimbledon.

The Arts

Hit songs are 'Bohemian Rhapsody' and 'Sailing'.

'One Flew Over the Cuckoo's Nest' starring Jack Nicholson wins five Oscars.

John Cleese appears in the English television series 'Fawlty Towers' for the first time.

Steven Spielberg's film 'Jaws' is released.

Left:
The United States government had maintained a military presence in South East Asia since 1946 with the intention of preventing communism spreading in the region. 50,000 Americans lost their lives in the disastrous Vietnam War.

1976

The Arts

Hit songs are 'Save Your Kisses for Me', 'Mississippi' and 'Don't Go Breaking My Heart'.

Sylvester Stallone stars in the film 'Rocky'.

The film 'Taxi Driver' is released starring Robert de Niro.

The Tate Gallery causes a stir when it exhibits 'Low Sculpture' – 120 bricks laid in an oblong.

Disco craze spreads throughout the US: it is claimed over 10,000 discos were open, compared to 1500 one year earlier.

Videogames are the latest craze, with Japanese company Atari sweeping the board.

TV series 'Charlie's Angels, shown first in autumn 1976, quickly take over the world.

Austrian body-builder and ex Mr Universe, Arnold Schwarzenegger gets his first movie role in 'Stay Hungry'.

'M*A*S*H' becomes top TV show.

World Events of 1976

Britain's new Prime Minister is James Callaghan.

Concorde makes its first commercial flight.

Racial violence erupts in South Africa.

Britain suffers its worst drought in 250 years.

American spacecraft 'Viking I' lands on Mars.

Jimmy Carter is elected President of the US.

The world's most violent earthquake for 12 years hits China.

In Uganda, Israeli commandos rescue 105 hostages at Entebbe Airport.

Huge bicentennial celebrations in the US help bring some pride back to the country after the Watergate saga and Richard Nixon's forced resignation.

The Queen opens Birmingham's £45 million National Exhibition Centre.

The Seychelles Islands become independent after 162 years of British rule.

Sporting Life

Austrian racing driver Niki Lauda is seriously injured in an accident in the German Grand Prix.

Rumanian gymnast Nadia Comaneci is awarded the first maximum score of 10.00 at the Olympics in Montreal.

Muhammad Ali announces his retirement from heavyweight boxing – not for the first or last time.

Winter Olympics were held in Innsbruck, Austria and the Summer Olympics in Montreal, Canada.

Top left:
Lawlessness and rioting spreads from Soweto to other areas such as the Alexandra Township, Natalspruit, Boksburg and townships around Johannesburg and Pretoria.

Centre left:
Jimmy Carter wins the November Presidential election bringing the Democrats back to the White House after an eight-year absence.

Left:
Fans and admirers all over the world were shocked to hear of the death of Elvis Presley at the age of 42.

Christmas is a time for reconciliation. A time not only for families and friends to come together but also for differences to be forgotten.

In 1976 I was reminded of the good that can flow from a friendship that is mended. Two hundred years ago the representatives of the 13 British colonies in North America signed the Declaration of Independence in Philadelphia.

This year we went to America to join in their bicentennial celebrations. Who would have thought 200 years ago that a descendant of King George III could have taken part in these celebrations.

Yet that same King was among the first to recognise that old scores must be settled and differences reconciled and the first United States Ambassador to Britain declared that he wanted "the old good nature and the old good humour restored".

And restored they were. The United States was born in bitter conflict with Britain, but we did not remain enemies for long.

From our reconciliation came incalculable benefits to mankind and a partnership which, together with many countries of the Commonwealth, was proved in two World Wars and ensured that the light of liberty was not extinguished.

King George III never saw the colonies he lost. My father, King George VI, was the first British Sovereign to see the famous skyline of Manhattan and to visit the rich and vibrant country that lies beyond it.

Wherever we went the welcome was the same, all the way to Boston, where the first shots in the war between Britain and America were fired.

Reconciliation, like the one that followed the American War of Independence, is the product of reason,

tolerance and love, and I think that Christmas is a good time to reflect on it. It is easy enough to see where reconciliation is needed and where it would heal and purify, obviously in national and international affairs, but also in homes and families.

It is not something that is easy to achieve. But things that are worth while seldom are, so it is encouraging to know that there are many people trying to achieve it.

A few weeks ago, for instance, I met in my home a group of people who are working for better understanding between people of different colour, different faiths and different philosophies and who are trying to solve the very real problems of community relations.

Another shining example is the peace movement in Northern Ireland. Here Roman Catholics and Protestants have joined together in a crusade of reconciliation to bring peace to the province.

Next year is a rather special one for me and I would like my silver jubilee year also to become a special one for people who find themselves the victims of human conflict.

The gift I would most value next year is that reconciliation should be found wherever it is needed, a reconciliation which would bring peace and security to families and neighbours at present suffering and torn apart.

Remember that good spreads outwards and every little does help. Mighty things from small beginnings grow, as indeed they grew from the small child of Bethlehem.

I believe there is another thought from which we can draw encouragement. If there is reconciliation – if we can get the climate right – the good effects will flow much more quickly than most people would believe possible.

Those who know the desert know also how quickly it can flower when the rains come. But who in Britain saw the parched earth and empty reservoirs last summer would have believed that the grass would grow so strong, so green, and so soon when the drought ended. When the conflict stops, peace can blossom just as quickly.

I wish you all a very happy Christmas and may the new year bring reconciliation between all people.

Right:
Queen Elizabeth II with her two sons Prince Andrew and Prince Edward shaking hands with the aircrew who flew them from Canada to England.

1977

World Events of 1977

Queen Elizabeth II celebrates her Silver Jubilee.

Refugees flee from Vietnam.

In South Africa, black rights leader Steve Biko dies in detention.

Spain holds its first democratic election for 41 years.

Uganda's Idi Amin holds 240 Americans hostage.

Gary Gilmore is the first convict to be executed in the US for ten years.

The average price for a house in London is £16,731.

The Spanish government requests entry into the EEC.

President Anwar Sadat becomes the first Arab leader to visit Israel.

The space shuttle 'Enterprise' makes its first free flight.

Richard Nixon admits, in a series of TV interviews with David Frost, that he "let the American people down".

Twenty-one-year old Steve Jobs launches his first Apple personal computer, quick to take the world by storm.

Sporting Life

'Red Rum' wins his third Grand National at Liverpool, England.

Nigel Short, England's chess prodigy, qualifies for a national chess final at the age of 11.

In football, Liverpool win the League for a record tenth time.

The Arts

The Pompidou Centre for the Arts opens in Paris.

Hit songs are 'When I Need You' and 'Don't Cry for Me, Argentina'.

The film 'Star Wars' takes a record $185 million at the box office.

Woody Allen stars in 'Annie Hall'.

The film 'Close Encounters of the Third Kind' is released.

'Saturday Night Fever' puts John Travolta and Olivia Newton-John on the map.

'Smokey and the Bandit' proves Burt Reynold's enduring fame.

'Roots" TV series becomes a fad, based on Alex Haley's book about his search for his African ancestors.

David Soul, one half of the detective double act 'Starsky and Hutch' scores a Number 1 hit with 'Don't Give Up On Us'.

The exceptionally well-organised exhibition of ancient Egyptian Pharaoh Tutankhamun sparks "pyramid power" fad which claims to harness spiritual energy through judicious placement of pyramids around the house.

Right:
Idi Amin was President of Uganda from 1971 until 1979, during which time around 300,000 Ugandan were murdered. He is known to have personally ordered the deaths of his political opponents.

Far right:
Red Rum winning the Grand National for the third time in April 1977.

I shall never forget the scene outside Buckingham Palace on Jubilee Day. The cheerful crowd was symbolic of the hundreds of thousands of people who greeted us wherever we went in this jubilee year, in 12 Commonwealth countries and 36 counties in the United Kingdom.

But I believe it also revealed to the world that we can be a united people. It showed that all the artificial barriers which divide man from man and family from family can be broken down. The street parties and village fetes, the presents, the flowers from the children, the mile upon mile of decorated streets and houses; these things suggest that the real value and pleasure of the celebration was that we all shared in it together.

Last Christmas I said that my wish for 1977 was that it should be a year of reconciliation. You have shown by the way in which you have celebrated the jubilee that this was not an impossible dream. Thank you all for your response. Nowhere is reconciliation more desperately needed than in Northern Ireland. That is why I was particularly pleased to go there. No one dared to promise an early end to the troubles, but there is no doubt that people of good will in Northern Ireland were greatly heartened with the rest of the nation and Commonwealth.

Many people in all parts of the world have demonstrated this good will in a practical way by giving to the Silver Jubilee Appeal. The results of their kindness will be appreciated by young people, and by those they are able to help, for many years to come.

The great resurgence of community spirit which has marked the celebrations has shown the value of the Christian ideal of loving our neighbours. If we can keep this spirit alive, life will become better for all of us.

The jubilee celebrations in London started with a service of thanksgiving in St Paul's Cathedral. To me this was a thanksgiving for all the good things for which our Commonwealth stands, the comradeship and cooperation it inspires and the friendship and tolerance it encourages. These are the qualities needed by all mankind.

The evening before the service I lit one small flame at Windsor and a chain of bonfires spread throughout Britain and on across the world to New Zealand and Australia. My hope this Christmas is that the Christian spirit of reconciliation may burn as strongly in our hearts during the coming year.

God bless you and a very happy Christmas to you all.

Left:
Queen Elizabeth II talking to well wishers in Camberwell during her silver jubilee year celebrations.

Right:
Queen Elizabeth II
laying a wreath
of poppies at the
Cenotaph,
watched by the
Prime Minister
and members of
the Government
on the 60th
anniversary of
the Armistice.

The birth of Christ gave us faith in the future. As I read through some earlier Christmas broadcasts I was struck by the way that this same idea – faith in the future – kept recurring.

You have heard three generations talking about the future. My grandfather could not have known what was in store for his grandchildren; yet his faith in the future gave him quiet confidence that the stern tests would be overcome. And so it has proved.

My father watched his grandchildren take their first steps. He knew that all the sacrifices and anxiety of the dark days of the war had been worthwhile. Now it is our turn to work for a future in which our grandchildren take their first steps one day.

We cannot be certain what lies ahead for them, but we should know enough to put them on the right path. We can do this if we have the good sense to learn from the experience of those who have gone before us and to hold on to all the good that has been handed down to us in trust.

Look around at your families as you are gathered together for Christmas. Look at the younger ones – they are the future and just as we were helped to understand and to appreciate the values of a civilised community it is now our responsibility to help them to do the same.

We must not let the difficulties of the present or the uncertainties of the future to cause us to lose faith. You remember the saying "The optimist proclaims that we live in the best of all possible worlds and the pessimist fears that this is true". It is far from easy to be cheerful and constructive when things around us suggest the opposite; but to give up the effort would mean, as it were, to switch off hope for a better tomorrow.

Even if the problems seem overwhelming there is always room for optimism.

Every problem presents us with the opportunity both to find an answer for ourselves and to help others.

The context of the lives of the next generation is being set, here and now, not so much by the legacy of science or wealth or political structure that we shall leave behind us, but by the example of our attitudes and behaviour to one another and by trying to show unselfish, loving and creative concern for those less fortunate than ourselves.

Christians have the compelling example of the life and teaching of Christ. For myself I would like nothing more than that my grandchildren should hold dear His ideals which have helped and inspired so many previous generations.

I wish you all, together with your children and grandchildren, a very happy Christmas.

World Events of 1978

A Polish cardinal becomes the Catholic Church's first ever non-Italian Pope since 1542.

The world's first air balloon crossing of the Atlantic is made.

The world's first test tube baby, Louise Brown, is born in Manchester.

Sweden becomes the first country to pass a law against aerosol sprays which affect the ozone layer.

South African journalist Donald Woods escapes to Lesotho.

Pieter Willem Botha is elected the new Prime Minister of South Africa.

US President Jimmy Carter brings Egypt's Anwar Sadat and Israel's Menachem Begin together at Camp David.

Sporting Life

The Ryder Cup is opened to European golfers, after more than 50 years as a match between the US and Great Britain.

Argentina wins football's World Cup.

The Arts

The film 'Superman' is released.

John Travolta and Olivia Newton-John star in the film 'Grease'.

Hit songs are 'Rivers of Babylon' and 'Summer Nights'.

Robert de Niro stars in the film 'The Deer Hunter'.

Andrew Lloyd Webber and Tim Rice's opera-musical 'Evita' is a hit.

Left:
Polish born Pope John Paul II is a champion for peace, justice, and human rights in the world and has won the respect of political leaders of all religious faiths. He was seriously injured in an attempted assassination in St. Peter's Square in 1981 and later visited his attacker, Mehmet Ali Agca, in prison to assure him of his forgiveness.

Far left:
Argentina hold the World Cup after beating Holland in the 1978 final.

1979

1979

Far right:
Ayatollah Khomeini, the Islamic fundamentalist was exiled to France in 1973 where he led a movement against the Shah of Iran. When the Shah left, Khomeini returned to lead the country.

Below centre:
The Afghan Marxist government requested the help of the USSR whose armies occupied the country in 1979. The ensuing war had little popular support in the USSR and was a major contribution to the collapse of the Soviet Union in 1991.

Right:
Margaret Thatcher greets the crowds as she celebrates her election win to become Britain's first women Prime Minister.

World Events of 1979

'Voyager I' discovers rings around Jupiter.
Israel and Egypt sign a peace treaty.
Margaret Thatcher is elected Britain's first woman Prime Minister.
The Sony Walkman comes on the market.
The Rubik's Cube goes on sale in the US.
Mother Teresa is awarded the Nobel Peace Prize.
Ayatollah Khomeini returns to Iran.
The Soviet Union invades Afghanistan.
Pope John Paul II visits the US.
Rhodesia is renamed Zimbabwe.
US President Jimmy Carter and Leonard Brezhnev sign the SALT Treaty.
With more than seventy million Americans claiming to be "born again" the Christian right or Moral Majority becomes a political force to be reckoned with in the US.
OPEC continues to inpose cuts in oil production leading to rationing in US.

The 77-ton Skylab breaks up as it re-enters earth's atmosphere over the Indian Ocean and Australia
An American Airlines DC-10 crashes in Chicago killing 275 people – the worst air disaster in US history.

Sporting Life

Spanish golfer Severiano Ballesteros wins the British Open.
Trevor Francis becomes Britain's first million-pound footballer.
British athlete Sebastian Coe breaks three world records (800 metres, 1,500 metres and the mile).
Nike's Tailwind shoe becomes the first air-cushioned athletic shoe on the market.

The Arts

Films released this year include Francis Ford Coppola's 'Apocalypse Now', starring Martin Sheen and Marlon Brando.
Hit songs are 'Heart of Glass' and 'Bright Eyes'.
Woody Allen stars in 'Manhattan'.

'Kramer vs. Kramer' is released, starring Meryl Streep and Dustin Hoffman.
Bob Dylan dismays his fans by converting to Christianity and releases 'Slow Train Coming'
Michael Jackson releases 'Off the Wall' his first solo album since the early seventies.

Every two years the heads of Government of the Commonwealth countries meet together to discuss matters of mutual interest.

This year they met in Africa and once again the meeting demonstrated the great value of personal contact and the desire of all the leaders to settle their differences in the friendly spirit of a family gathering.

In this Year of the Child people all over the world have been asked to give particular thought to the special needs of sick and handicapped children, to the hungry and homeless and to those in trouble or distress wherever they may be found.

It is an unhappy coincidence that political and economic forces have made this an exceptionally difficult and tragic year for many families and children in several parts of the world, but particularly in South-east Asia.

The situation has created a desperately serious challenge and I am glad to know that so many people of the Commonwealth have responded with wonderful generosity and kindness.

It seems that the greater the needs of children, the more people everywhere rise to the occasion.

At Christmas we give presents to each other. Let us also stop to think whether we are making enough effort to pass on our experience of life to our children.

Left:
Queen Elizabeth II meets a child dressed as a clown in Hyde Park.

Above:
Queen Elizabeth II and Prince Andrew with the Mayor of Dar es Salaam at the Municipal Buildings watching dancers during the Royal visit of East Africa.

Left:
Queen Elizabeth II with Prince Philip and her sons Prince Edward, Prince Charles the Prince of Wales and Prince Andrew the Prince of York.

1980

World Events of 1980

* Sanjay Gandhi, son of India's Prime Minister, dies in a plane crash.
* Mount St Helens erupts in the US
* The SAS rescues 19 hostages from the Iranian embassy in London.
* Two years of drought bring famine to East Africa.
* Former Hollywood actor Ronald Reagan is elected President of the US.
* 3,000 die in Italian earthquake.
* The US boycott the Olympic Games in Moscow in protest against the Soviet Union's invasion of Afghanistan.
* 'Voyager ' sends pictures of Saturn to earth.
* Margaret Thatcher declares she is "not for turning".
* The wreck of the 'Titanic' is located.
* An airborne attempt to rescue American hostages in Iran ends in disaster which will lead to President Carter's disgrace.
* 1980 was also the year of the Pac-Man, the most popular arcade game yet.

DAILY Mirror THE NORTH'S BIGGEST DAILY SALE
SPECIAL ISSUE

JOHN LENNON shot dead in New York Dec 8, 1980
DEATH OF A HERO
PLEASE TURN TO PAGES TWO and THREE

Sporting Life

* British athletes Sebastian Coe and Steve Ovett win Olympic gold medals.
* Bjorn Borg wins Wimbledon for the fifth time.
* Welsh boxer Johnny Owen dies after a title fight against Mexico's Lupe Pintor.
* Winter Olympics take place in Lake Placid, New York State.

The Arts

* Steve McQueen loses his battle against cancer.
* John Lennon is shot dead.
* John Hurt plays 'The Elephant Man'.
* Britain apologises to Saudi Arabia for the TV programme, 'Death of a Princess.'
* British TV audiences are hooked on 'Dallas'.
* Dan Ackroyd and John Belushi bring their R&B loving characters to the screen in 'Blues Brothers'.
* 'Urban Cowboy', starring John Travolta, starts a brief new western fad.
* 'The Empire Strikes Back', the second film in the Star Wars trilogy, was huge hit.
* 'Who Shot JR?' was the most important question of late 1980 as 'Dallas' fever reached its peak.

Top:
President Carter's raid on Iran to free 53 American hostages ends in disaster. "Blue Light Squad" are forced to land in a remote desert in the East of Iran and sustain tragic casualties before aborting the operation and flying out, leaving the desert sands littered with burnt-out planes and the bodies of their colleagues.

Centre:
The former Beatle John Lennon was shot dead in New York City on December 8th.

Far left:
President Carter at the US Democratic Convention in New York. The aborted rescue mission to free American hostages in Iran will lead to his disgrace and fall from power.

Above:
The Queen Mother celebrates her 80th birthday in the company of her daughter Queen Elizabeth II.

I was glad that the celebrations of my mother's eightieth birthday last summer gave so much pleasure. I wonder whether you remember, during the thanksgiving service in St Paul's, the congregation singing that wonderful hymn, "Immortal, Invisible, God only wise":

Now give us we pray thee the spirit of love,
The gift of true wisdom that comes from above,
The spirit of service that has naught of pride,
The gift of true courage, and thee as our guide.

Did you catch the words of that hymn? The spirit of service that has naught of pride.

The gift of true courage, and thee as our guide.

The loyalty and affection which so many people showed to my mother reflected a feeling, expressed in many different ways, that she is a person who has given selfless service to the people of this country and of the Commonwealth.

As I go about the country and abroad I meet many people who, all in their own ways, are making a real contribution to their community. I come across examples of unselfish service in all walks of life and in many unexpected places.

Some people choose their occupation so that they can spend their lives in the service of their fellow citizens. We see doctors, nurses and hospital staff caring for the sick; those in the churches and religious communities, in central and local government, in the Armed Services, in the police and in the courts and prisons, in industry and commerce. It is the same urge to make a contribution which drives those seeking the highest standards in education or art, in music or architecture.

Others find ways to give service in their spare time, through voluntary organisations or simply on their own individual initiative, contributing in a thousand ways to all that is best in our society. It may be providing company for the old and house-bound, help for the disabled, care for the deprived and those in trouble, concern for neighbours or encouragement for the young.

To all of you on this Christmas Day, whatever your conditions of work and life, easy or difficult, whether you feel that you are achieving something or whether you feel frustrated, I want to say a word of thanks. And I include all those who don't realise that they deserve thanks and are content that what they do is unseen and unrewarded. The very act of living a decent and upright life is in itself a positive factor in maintaining civilised standards.

We face grave problems in the life of our country, but our predecessors, and many alive today, have faced far greater difficulties, both in peace and war, and have overcome them by courage and calm determination. They never lost hope and they never lacked confidence in themselves or in their children.

In difficult times we may be tempted to find excuses for self-indulgence and to wash our hands of responsibility. Christmas stands for the opposite. The Wise Men and the shepherds remind us that it is not enough simply to do our jobs; we need to go out and look for opportunities to help those less fortunate than ourselves, even if that service demands sacrifice. It was their belief and confidence in God which inspired them to visit the stable and it is this unselfish will to serve that will see us through the difficulties we face.

We know that the world can never be free from conflict and pain, but Christmas also draws our attention to all that is hopeful and good in this changing world; it speaks of values and qualities that are true and permanent and it reminds us that the world we would like to see can only come from the goodness of the heart.

When you hear the bells ringing at Christmas, think of the lines written by Tennyson:

Ring out false pride in place and blood,
The civic slander and the spite;
Ring in the love of truth and right,
Ring in the common love of good. ...
Ring in the valiant man and free,
The larger heart, the kindlier hand,
Ring out the darkness of the land.
Ring in the Christ that is to be.

To all of you wherever you may be, I wish happiness this Christmas.

Last July we had the joy of seeing our eldest son married amid scenes of great happiness, which made 1981 a very special year for us. The wonderful response the wedding evoked was very moving.

Just before that there had been a very different scene in the garden at Buckingham Palace when 3,500 disabled people, with their families, came to tea with us. And, with members of my family, I have just met some more disabled people who came here to receive special cars which will give them the mobility they so desperately need. We handed over the keys of the new cars and also talked to handicapped people who have had their cars for some time.

The International Year of Disabled People has performed a very real service by focusing attention on their problems. We have all become more aware of them and I am sure that many of you, like myself, have been impressed by the courage they show.

Below:
Queen Elizabeth II on a visit to Essex receives a model of Prince Charles and Lady Diana for their wedding from disabled Agnes Stevens.

There are, of course, many aspects of courage. There is the physical courage shown in war. Chesterton described it as "almost a contradiction in terms … a strong desire to live taking the form of a readiness to die". It is sobering and inspiring to remember what man will do for an ideal in which he believes. Bravery of this kind is shown in peace as well as in war. The Armed Forces and the police are showing it every day.

So are the fire services, ambulance drivers, members of the public and even children, and the courage of the bomb disposal experts fills us with awe.

All around us we see these acts of selflessness, people putting the life of someone else before their own.

Then there is perseverance – sticking to the job. This is how the disabled have learnt to cope with life, becoming better people in the process, and their courage in handling their difficulties and in many cases living an almost normal life, on making abnormal life normal, shows our own problems to be insignificant by comparison.

It is not only the disabled who are showing day-to-day perseverance and courage.

This Christmas we should remember especially the people of Northern Ireland, who are attempting to live ordinary lives in times of strain and conflict; the unemployed who are trying to maintain their self-respect without work and to care for their families; and those from other parts of the Commonwealth who have come to Britain to make new lives but have not yet found themselves fully accepted.

Perhaps the greatest contribution of the disabled is to give the inspiration and incentive to do more to help others. From this we can gain the strength to try to do that little bit extra, as individuals, as members of our families, and as nations.

We have seen in 1981 how many individuals have devoted themselves to trying to make life more tolerable for handicapped people, by giving loving care and by providing money and effort to improve facilities and to hasten research. There are 450 million disabled people in the world but wonderful work is being done in the prevention and cure of disablement. Diseases like polio and measles can be controlled by a very cheap multiple vaccine.

In the last 12 years the Royal Commonwealth Society for the Blind has restored sight to over one million Commonwealth citizens. But throughout this century there have been great advances in the awakening of conscience and concern for our fellow human beings. Governments now regard it as their duty to try to protect their people, through social services, from the worst effects of illness, bereavement, joblessness and disability.

We are also trying to reach beyond a nation's responsibility for its citizens. There is a wide disparity between the wealth of nations and I have found that there is a spirit of eagerness to redress this throughout the world.

I have spoken of courage in its different forms and of the effect a display of courage can have on the world in which we live.

Ultimately, however, we accept in our hearts that most important of all is moral courage. As human beings we generally know what is right and how we should act and speak. But we are also very aware of how difficult it is to have the courage of our convictions. Our Christian faith helps us to sustain those convictions.

Christ not only revealed to us the truth in his teaching. He lived by what he believed and gave us the strength to try to do the same – and finally on the cross, he showed the supreme example of physical and moral courage. That sacrifice was the dawn of Christianity and this is why at Christmas time we are inspired by the example of Christ as we celebrate his birth.

A few weeks ago I was sent this poem:
*When all your world is torn with grief
and strife,
Think yet – when there seems nothing
left to men,
The frail and timeworn fabric of your
life,
The golden thread of courage has no
end.*

So to you all I say "God bless you and a very happy Christmas".

1981

World Events of 1981

* The Prince of Wales marries Lady Diana Spencer.
* In China, Mao Tse-tung's widow is condemned for her part in the Cultural Revolution.
* An attempt is made to assassinate President Reagan.
* Race riots hit many towns in Britain.
* Martial law is imposed in Poland following strikes and demonstrations.
* The first cases of AIDS among homosexuals and drug users are identified in American cities.
* The guillotine is abolished in France.
* The stock market suffers the second worst fall in its history.
* IRA hunger striker Bobby Sands is elected an MP but dies a few weeks later, provoking riots.

Sporting Life

* Torvill and Dean become European ice dancing champions.
* Bob Champion, who was diagnosed with cancer and given 8 months to live, wins Grand National.
* England wins the test series 3 – 1 against Australia.
* Steve Davis wins the world snooker championships.

The Arts

* 'Brideshead Revisited' is serialised on British television.
* 'Cats', a ballet-musical by Andrew Lloyd Webber, hits the London stage.
* 'Chariots Of Fire' and 'The French Lieutenants Woman' were released.
* Hit songs are 'Stand and Deliver' and 'Imagine'.

Above: Egyptian President Mohammed Anwar el Sadat was murdered by Islamic fundamentalist gunmen in the middle of an annual military parade, as they opened fire on the president and his party. He was killed along with five others.

Left:
Millions around the world watched on TV as the Prince of Wales and Lady Diana Spencer made their vows in St. Paul's Cathedral. The crowds that gathered around Buckingham Palace were treated to the customary appearance of the couple on the balcony with members of the Royal family, and a memorable and very public embrace.

1982

World Events of 1982

* Mark Thatcher, son of the British Prime Minister, goes missing in the Sahara Desert.
* Unemployment in Britain is above 3 million.
* Britain goes to war with Argentina over the Falkland Islands.
* The Princess of Wales gives birth to her first son, Prince William.
* Henry VIII's flagship, the 'Mary Rose', which sank in the Solent in 1545 with great loss of life, is raised from the sea-bed.
* Princess Grace of Monaco, formerly actress Grace Kelly, dies in a car crash.
* Peace keeping troops from the US, France and Italy are sent to Beirut. British troops join them later.
* Spain gives up its claim to Gibraltar.
* The first test-tube twins are born in Cambridge.
* Sophia Loren goes to jail for tax evasion.

Sporting Life

* Tom Watson became the fifth man to win both the British and US Open Golf Championships in the same year.
* Italy wins the World Cup, beating West Germany 3 – 1 in Madrid.
* Ian Botham achieves his highest Test score of 208 against India.
* Martina Navratilova and Jimmy Connors are Wimbledon champions.

The Arts

* Mrs Mary Whitehouse fails in her attempt to bring a private prosecution against Michael Bogdanov for a scene in the National Theatre play 'The Romans in Britain'.
* Channel Four goes on the air.
* Jacques Tati of M Hulot fame dies.
* Henry Fonda dies just 2 weeks after winning his first Oscar.

Below:
The Prince and Princess of Wales with their first son, Prince William.

Below:
More than 250 British and 650 Argentines were killed in the conflict over the Falkland Islands. Argentina has never renounced their claim to sovereignty over the territory.

It is 50 years since the BBC External Service was started and my grandfather King George V made the first Christmas broadcast from Sandringham.

Today I am speaking to you from the library at Windsor Castle, in a room which was once occupied by Queen Elizabeth I. This is my home, where for many years now my family and I have celebrated Christmas.

Within a few feet of where I am standing is the cliff, with its wonderful commanding view over the Thames, which led William the Conqueror to build a castle on this ideal defensive position – a castle which has to this day been the home of Kings and Queens.

In October I was in Brisbane for the Commonwealth Games and then went by sea in 'Britannia' to visit a number of those beautiful Commonwealth island countries in the Pacific.

At first sight, there does not appear to be much connection between a Norman castle, this Elizabethan gallery, the Commonwealth Games and the Pacific Islands. But in fact they are all linked by the sea. William became the Conqueror after invading England by sea.

It was the voyages of discovery by the great seamen of Queen Elizabeth's day which laid the foundations of modern trade, and to this day 90 per cent of it still goes by sea.

Discovery and trade in their turn laid the foundations of the present day Commonwealth.

It was the development of ocean-going passenger vessels that allowed the peoples of the world to move about and get to know each other.

Such names as Drake, Anson, Frobisher, Cook, Vancouver and Phillip are familiar to people in widely different parts of the Commonwealth – while in Britain we owe our independence to the seamen who fought the Armada nearly 400 years ago and to Nelson and his Band of Brothers who destroyed Napoleon's dreams of invasion.

Nor could the great battles for peace and freedom in the first half of the 20th century have been won without control of the seas.

Earlier this year in the South Atlantic the Royal Navy and the Merchant Navy enabled our sailors, soldiers and airmen to go to the rescue of the Falkland Islanders 8,000 miles across the ocean; and to reveal the professional skills and courage that could be called on in defence of basic freedoms.

Throughout history, seamen all over the world have shared a common experience and there is a special sense of brotherhood between merchant and naval seamen, fishermen, life-boatmen and, more recently, yachtsmen.

The navigators from the Pacific Islands, the fishermen of the Indian Ocean and China seas, and the men who man the oil rig supply ships in the North Atlantic have all learnt to come to terms with the varying moods of the seas and oceans.

In much the same way, the members of the Commonwealth, which evolved from Britain's seafaring history, have acquired an affinity through sharing a common philosophy of individual freedom, democratic government and the rule of law.

It may not sound very substantial but when measured against the number and variety of inter-Commonwealth organisations and the multitude of commercial, medical, legal and sporting connections, it becomes clear that this common philosophy has had a very powerful influence for unity.

Nothing could have demonstrated this unity more vividly than the immensely reassuring support given to Britain by the Commonwealth during the Falkland Islands crisis.

But the Commonwealth reveals its strength in many different ways. Any of you who attended or watched the events at the Commonwealth Games at Brisbane cannot have failed to notice the unique atmosphere of friendly rivalry and the generous applause for all the competitors.

In a world more concerned with argument, disagreement and violence, the Games stand out as a demonstration of the better side of human nature and of the great value of the Commonwealth as an association of free and independent nations.

The Games also illustrated the consequences of the movement of peoples within the Commonwealth. Colour is no longer an indication of national origin. Until this century most racial and religious groups remained concentrated in their homelands but today almost every country of the Commonwealth has become multi-racial and multi-religious.

This change has not been without its difficulties, but I believe that for those with a sense of tolerance the arrival and proximity of different races and religions have provided a much better chance for each to appreciate the value of the others.

At this time of the year, Christians celebrate the birth of their Saviour, but no longer in an exclusive way. We hope that our greetings at Christmas to all people of religious conviction and goodwill will be received with the same understanding that we try to show in receiving the greetings of other religious groups at their special seasons.

The poet John Donne said, "No man is an island, entire of itself; every man is a piece of the continent, a part of the main."

That is the message of the Commonwealth it is also the Christian message. Christ attached supreme importance to the individual and he amazed the world in which he lived by making it clear that the unfortunate and the under-privileged had an equal Heaven with the rich and powerful.

But he also taught that man must do his best to live in harmony with man and to love his neighbours. In the Commonwealth, we are all neighbours and it is with this thought in mind that I wish you all, wherever you may be, the blessings of a happy and peaceful Christmas

Right:
Queen Elizabeth II with Indira Ghandi and Prince Philip during the Royal Tour of India.

In the year I was born, radio communication was barely out of its infancy: there was no television: civil aviation had hardly started and space satellites were still in the realm of science fiction.

When my grandfather visited India in 1911, it took three weeks by sea to get there, last month I flew back from Delhi to London in a matter of hours, it took King George V three months to make the round trip.

In two thirds of that time Prince Philip and I were able to visit Jamaica, Mexico, the United States and Canada in the winter, followed by Sweden in the summer, and ending up in the autumn with Kenya, Bangladesh and finally India for the Commonwealth heads of government meeting in New Delhi.

Travel and communication have entered a completely new dimension.

In Los Angeles I went to see the Space-Shuttle which is playing such an important part in providing more and better international telecommunications.

One of the tasks of that Space-Shuttle was to launch an Indian telecommunications and weather satellite and last month I was able to see how this operated during our visit to an earth station in New Delhi.

All this astonishing and very rapid development has changed the lives of almost everyone.

Leaders and specialists can meet and discuss political and technical problems: news travels faster and there is more of it: new opportunities for world trade and commerce have been opened up by this communication revolution: perhaps more important, modern technology has touched most aspects of life throughout the world.

We saw this in dramatic form in India. Twenty-two years ago I had seen something of the problems facing this vast country, but since then the population has grown from 440 million to over 700 million.

Yet India has managed to become one of the ten or so leading industrial nations in the world and has become self-sufficient in food.

But in spite of all the progress that has been made the greatest problem in the world today remains the gap between rich and poor countries and we shall not begin to close this gap until we hear less about nationalism and more about inter-dependence.

One of the main aims of the Commonwealth is to make an effective contribution towards redressing the economic balance between nations.

What we want to see is still more modern technology being used by poorer countries to provide employment and to produce primary products and components, which will be bought in turn by the richer countries at competitive prices.

I have therefore been heartened by the real progress that is being made through the Commonwealth technical cooperation fund and various exchange schemes.

Britain and other richer Commonwealth countries run aid schemes and these are very important, but the key word for the Commonwealth is cooperation.

There is a flow of experts in all directions, with Canadians helping in the Caribbean, Indians in Africa, New Zealanders in India, Australians in Papua New Guinea, British in Kenya, the list is endless.

The web of contacts provided by the Commonwealth is an intricate pattern based on self help and cooperation.

Yet in spite of these advances the age-old problems of human communication are still with us.

We have the means of sending and receiving messages, we can travel to meetings in distant parts of the world, we can exchange experts: but we still have difficulty in finding the right messages to send, we can still ignore the messages we do not like to hear and we can still talk in riddles and listen without trying to comprehend.

Perhaps even more serious is the risk that this mastery of technology may blind us to the more fundamental needs of people. Electronics cannot create comradeship: computers cannot generate compassion: satellites cannot transmit tolerance.

And no amount of technology could have engineered the spirit of the Commonwealth that was so evident in Delhi or the frank, friendly and understanding communication that such a spirit makes possible.

I hope that Christmas will remind us all that it is not how we communicate but what we communicate with each other that really matters.

We in the Commonwealth are fortunate enough to belong to a worldwide comradeship. Let us make the most of it: let us all resolve to communicate as friends in tolerance and understanding.

Only then can we make the message of the angels come true: "Peace on earth, goodwill towards men".

I always look forward to being able to talk to everyone at Christmas time, and at the end of another year I again send you all my warmest greetings.

1983

World Events of 1983

* Attempts are made to divert the flow of lava from the active Mount Etna.
* British voters re-elect Margaret Thatcher in a landslide victory for the Tory party.
* Cecil Parkinson is forced to resign over his affair with Sara Keays.
* 134 IRA prisoners break out of the Maze prison.
* Gold bars worth £25 million were stolen from the Brinks-Mat ware house at Heathrow.
* In the US, Martin Luther King's birthday is declared a national holiday.
* Polish Solidarity leader Lech Walesa is awarded the Nobel Prize for Peace.
* The Walton Sextuplets, all girls, are born in Liverpool.
* A car bomb in Beirut destroys the US embassy.
* Compact discs go on sale.
* The invasion of the small Caribbean island of Grenada by the US did wonders for President Reagan's approval ratings in the polls.
* Cabbage patch doll craze sweeps the world. No two of these pudgy, stuffed-cloth dolls looks exactly alike: their hand-made construction meant that supplies were limited and kept prices high.
* A truck loaded with high explosives destroys the US Marine headquaters in Beirut, killing 241.
* The US places its first cruise mis siles in the UK.

Sporting Life

* Bjorn Borg retires from tennis at the age of 26.
* Geoff Boycott is sacked by Yorkshire Cricket Club.
* In yachting, Australia wins the America's Cup.

Left:
Sixty-eight people died and more than 100 were injured in a sucide bomb attack against the US Embassy in Beirut on April 18th .

* England beat Luxembourg 4 – 0, but fail to qualify for the European finals.

The Arts

* A symphony by Mozart, composed when he was 9, is discovered in Denmark.
* The British composer, Sir William Walton, dies.
* 'Gandhi', a British film directed by Richard Attenborough, wins eight Oscars.
* 'Every breath you take' by Police, was a hit.

* MrT crashes in on his popularity as star of the 'A Team'.
* 'The Return of the Jedi', 'Terms of Endearment' and 'The Big Chill' starring Tom Cruise are the other big films of the year.
* 'Thriller' by Michael Jackson was the biggest music release of the year.
* The big new sound is however povided by REM, who's first LP 'Murmur' is a huge hit with college and university students.

Last June, we celebrated the fortieth anniversary of D-Day. That occasion in Normandy was a memorable one for all of us who were able to be there.

It was partly a day of sadness, as we paid our respects to those who died for us, but it was also a day full of comradeship and of hope.

Above:
Queen Elizabeth II meets the Emir of Bahrain.

Right:
Queen Elizabeth II together with Ronald Reagan at Utah Beach Normandy, for the 40th D Day Anniversary Ceremony.

For me, perhaps the most lasting impression was one of thankfulness that the forty intervening years have been ones of comparative peace.

The families of those who died in battle, and the veterans who fought beside them in their youth, can take comfort from the fact that the great nations of the world have contrived, sometimes precariously maybe, to live together without major conflict.

The grim lessons of two world wars have not gone completely unheeded.

I feel that in the world today there is too much concentration on the gloomy side of life, so that we tend to underestimate our blessings. But I think we can at least feel thankful that in spite of everything, our children and grandchildren are growing up in a more or less peaceful world.

The happy arrival of our fourth grandchild gave great cause for family celebrations. But, for parents and grandparents, a birth is also a time for reflection on what the future holds for the baby and how they can best ensure its safety and happiness.

To do that, I believe we must be prepared to learn as much from them as they do from us. We could use some of that sturdy confidence and devastating honesty with which children rescue us from self-doubts and self-delusions.

We could borrow that unstinting trust of the child in its parents for our dealings with each other.

Above all, we must retain the child's readiness to forgive, with which we are all born and which it is all too easy to lose as we grow older. Without it, divisions between families, communities and nations remain unbridgeable.

We owe it to our children and grandchildren to live up to the standards of behaviour and tolerance which we are so eager to teach them.

One of the more encouraging developments since the war has been the birth of the Commonwealth. Like a child, it has grown, matured and strengthened, until today the vision of its future is one of increasing understanding and co-operation between its members.

Notwithstanding the strains and stresses of nationalism, different cultures and religions and its growing membership, the Commonwealth family has still managed to hold together and to make a real contribution to the prevention of violence and discord.

And it is not only in the Commonwealth that progress has been made towards a better understanding between nations. The enemies of 1944, against whom so many of our countrymen fought and died on those beaches in Normandy, are now our steadfast friends and allies.

But friendship, whether we are talking of continents or next door neighbours, should not need strife as its forerunner.

It is particularly at Christmas, which marks the birth of the Prince of Peace, that we should work to heal old wounds and to abandon prejudice and suspicion. What better way of making a start than by remembering what Christ said: "Except ye become as little children, ye shall not enter into the kingdom of heaven".

God bless you, and a very happy Christmas to you all – to parents and children, grandchildren and, of course, great-grandchildren.

1984

World Events of 1984

* An astronaut takes the first untethered space walk from the US space shuttle 'Challenger'.
* The USSR and all Eastern European countries except Romania, boycott the Los Angeles Olympic Games.
* The BMX (bicycle motorcross) craze hits Britain.
* An IRA bomb devastates the Grand Hotel in Brighton where the Tories have gathered for their annual conference.
* "Baby Fae" is given a baboon's heart in an attempt to save her life.
* Desmond Tutu is given the Nobel Peace Prize.
* Ronald Reagan is re-elected to a second term as US President.
* The scale of the Ethiopian famine is exposed by TV journalist Michael Buerk.
* Indira Gandhi is assassinated by her Sikh bodyguards.
* The cause of AIDS is identified as a retrovirus named HIV (Human Immunodeficiency Virus). Government awareness campaigns are launched.

Above: The Welsh Actor Richard Burton (1926-1984) seen here with Elizabeth Taylor, whom he married twice, died at the age of 58.

Left:
During the 1970s 80s and 90s a campaign of terror and assassination was operated by the Provisional IRA and there were attempts on British subjects lives in Northern Ireland, the British mainland and in other countries. In October 1984 they tried to kill Margaret Thatcher and members of her Cabinet with a 20lb bomb planted in the Grand Hotel in Brighton where most of them were staying. The Prime Minister had a narrow escape. Four people died and many were injured.

Sporting Life

* Mary Decker trips over Zola Budd's heel in the 3,000 metres Olympic final.
* Carl Lewis wins four gold medals in Los Angeles.
* John McEnroe beats Jimmy Connors to win the men's singles final at Wimbledon.
* Martina Navratilova takes the women's title for the fifth time – and her third in succession.

The Arts

* Actor Richard Burton dies.
* 'Do they know it's Christmas?' tops the charts and raises millions for the starving.
* Michael Jackson's 'Thriller' topped 37 million in sales.
* 'The Terminator' and 'Canan the Destroyer' turn Arnold Schwarzenegger into a superstar.
* Eddie Murphy establishes his comic genius as he stars in Beverly Hills Cops.
* 'Indiana Jones and the Temple of Doom' launches the first of a series of Indiana Jones films.
* Prince rules the music scene with 'Purple Rain'.
* Bruce Springsteen's 'Born in the USA' establishes him as the "all-American" rock star.
* The Cosby Show, starring already hugely successful comedian Bill Cosby, is first aired: it will become the most successful TV sitcom of the eighties.

1985

World Events of 1985

* Terry Waite frees four British hostages in Libya.
* The "Baby Cotton" surrogacy case is settled in the High Court.
* Mikhail Gorbachev becomes the new Soviet leader.
* Bangladesh is battered by a cyclone and tidal wave.
* 41 die as British football hooligans riot in Heysel, Belgium.
* Clive Sinclair unveils his C5, saying that by 2000, the petrol-powered engine will be a thing of the past.
* The pound fell to its lowest value ever – close to $1.
* 13 year old Ruth Lawrence wins a first class honours degree in Maths at Oxford.
* BBC journalists strike. The World Service is silent for one day.
* French secret agents sink the Greenpeace ship 'Rainbow Warrior'.
* Only 1 in 3 Britons now smoke.

Sporting Life

* Tony Jacklin wins the Ryder Cup.
* Zola Budd sets a new world record of 48.07 seconds in the 5,000 metres.
* Manchester United win the English FA Cup Final.
* 17-year-old unseeded Boris Becker wins Wimbledon.

The Arts

* 'Live Aid' raises £40 million.
* 'Like a Virgin' is a hit for Madonna.
* Poets Robert Graves and Philip Larkin die.
* 'Les Miserables' is a stage hit.

Below:
Bob Geldof was so moved by the plight of refugees in Ethiopia that he organised the Live Aid concert to raise money to feed the starving.

The people who have won awards in their work come from all walks of life and they don't blow their trumpets: so unless, like me, you are able to read the citations describing what they have done, you couldn't begin to guess at some of the remarkable stories that lie behind their visits to the palace.

Six people were chosen as representatives of the 2,000 who get such awards each year. And some of those who appeared in the broadcast beamed by satellite to Europe for the first time did not know of their inclusion until Christmas Eve.

But such heroism and service was not the only way to make good news.

There were also people who had helped companies win the Queen's Awards for Exports and Technology – like the darts firm with just five employees which exported to 40 countries. They were so enterprising that they introduced the game of darts into places where it had never been played.

Above:
Queen Elizabeth II attends a Royal Variety Show in London.

Above right:
Queen Elizabeth II meets Wayne Sleep at the Royal Variety Show in London.

Right:
Queen Elizabeth II with her Family.

Christmas is a time of good news. I believe it is a time to look at the good things of life and to remember that there are a great many people trying to make the world a better place.

We should never forget our obligation to make our own individual contributions, however small, towards the sum of human goodness.

Looking at the morning newspapers, listening to the radio and watching television it is only too easy to conclude that nothing is going right in the world.

It used to be said that "no news is good news" but today you might well think that "good news is no news".

The Queen was yesterday said to be delighted with the new look given to her annual Christmas message by a team of BBC film makers led by Sir David Attenborough.

The message, transmitted around the world by satellite, was a break from the normally formal Queen's broadcast delivered from her desk at Buckingham Palace.

The Queen emphasised traditional Christian values, and recalled the meaning of the Christmas story.

But the presentation was thoroughly contemporary, with the Queen, in tweed coat and relaxed mood, seen attending the annual Christmas party for the children of Palace employees as Father Christmas arrived, escorted by pipers, in a horse-drawn sleigh.

The Queen was shown taking the children on a tour of the *Royal Mews*. She also showed them the horses that had pulled the carriages at last summer's Royal Wedding. As a choir sang "Away in a Manger", the Queen turned to the camera to deliver the formal part of her message.

She said: "For the children, the party and the meeting with Father Christmas, are perhaps the most exciting part of the evening. But I hope that a walk through the stables also helps bring the traditional Christmas story alive for them.

"I hope it also helps them to realise how fortunate they are to have comfortable homes and warm beds to go to, unlike the Holy family, who had to share with the animals because there was no room at the inn."

"It is no easy task to bring up children, "whether you are famous or quite unknown," but we can all help by letting the spirit of Christmas fill our homes with love and care and by heeding our Lord's injunction to treat others as you would like them to treat you."

The 10-minute film was the first to be produced by Sir David Attenborough, the naturalist and broadcaster. Sir David was selected by the Queen for the assignment in September, after the death of Mr Richard Cawston, who made the film 'The Royal Family' in 1969 and had produced 15 annual Christmas messages.

Broadcasters said yesterday that Sir David's production was the first to make full use of contemporary television techniques.

Among the innovations was the decision to make the film virtually at the last minute, to produce a seasonal flavour. Filming was on December 18.

In the past, the film was made in early December, to allow time for film to be shipped by air to the scores of countries where the Queen's message is televised.

Right:
Queen Elizabeth II and Prince Philip: the official portrait to celebrate her 60th birthday.

Below:
Queen Elizabeth II meets children and crowds at Buckingham Palace, London.

1986

Left:
Prince Andrew, the Queen's second son, married Sarah Ferguson on 23 July 1986. They were given the titles Duke and Duchess of York.

World Events of 1986
* US space shuttle explodes on take-off.
* Plans for a Channel Tunnel are announced.
* Corazon Aquino becomes President of the Philippines.
* The Duchess of Windsor, formerly Mrs Simpson, dies.
* A nuclear reactor explodes at Chernobyl.
* Soviet dissident Andrei Sakharov is freed.
* Harold Macmillan ("Supermac") dies aged 92.
* Irish people vote against divorce.

* Prince Andrew marries Sarah Ferguson.
* The Queen and the Duke of Edinburgh visit China.
* Prince Charles admits on TV that he talks to his plants.
* Divers discover the cause of the 'Titanic' disaster in 1912.

Sporting Life
* Mike Tyson becomes the youngest to win the WBC world heavyweight title.
* Richard Branson crosses the Atlantic in record time in 'Virgin Atlantic Challenger II'.

* English cricketer Ian Botham admits smoking cannabis and gets a 2-month ban.
* Joe Johnson wins the Embassy World Snooker Championship as a 150 – 1 outsider.

The Arts
* Nigerian writer Wole Soyinka wins the Nobel Prize for Literature.
* Sculptor Henry Moore dies.
* Pop singer Boy George is convicted of possessing heroin.

Right:
The car ferry, Herald of Free Enterprise began to list and keeled over, coming to rest on a sandbank, shortly after leaving the port of Zeebrugge. An inquiry concluded that the accident was due to water flooding the car deck after the bow doors had been left open.

World Events of 1987

* Terry Waite is kidnapped in Beirut.
* Gorbachev announces reforms – perestroika (reconstruction) and glasnost (openness).
* Weathermen fail to forecast a hurricane which leaves a trail of destruction across southern England.
* The Church of England's General Synod vote in favour of the ordination of women.
* Mrs Thatcher is elected for a third term.
* Los Angeles is rocked by an earthquake.
* More than 70 nations have agreed on measures to protect the ozone layer.
* The 'Herald of Free Enterprise' sinks off Zeebrugge.
* The Duchess of Windsor's jewellery fetches £31m at auction.

Sporting Life

* Irish cyclist Steven Roche wins the Tour de France.
* Ben Johnson sets a new world record of 9.83 seconds in the 100 metres.
* Tottenham Hotspur's own goal gives Coventry a 3 – 2 win in the FA Cup.
* Nigel Mansell wins the British Grand Prix.

The Arts

* Andy Warhol dies.
* Enid Blyton's 'Noddy' stories are to be revised to make them politically correct.
* 'Crocodile Dundee' is a box office hit.
* Mary Whitehouse attacks the soap 'Eastenders'.
* One of Mozart's notebooks fetches £2.3 million at auction.

Right:
Queen Elizabeth II inspecting the Scots Guards at Buckingham Palace.

Sooner or later we all become aware of the passing of the years, but every now and then we get a sharp reminder that time is moving on rather quicker than we expected. This happened to me last month when we celebrated our 40th wedding anniversary. I was very touched that so many of you were kind enough to send messages of good wishes.

There is no point in regretting the passage of time. Growing older is one of the facts of life, and it has its own compensations. Experience should help us to take a more balanced view of events and to be more understanding about the foibles of human nature.

Like everyone else, I learn about what is going on in the world from the media, but I am fortunate to have another source of information. Every day hundreds of letters come to my desk, and I make a point of reading as many of them as I possibly can.

The vast majority are a pleasure to read. There are also sad ones from people who want help, there are interesting ones from people who want to tell me what they think about current issues or who have suggestions to make about changing the way things are done.

Below:
Prince Charles and Princess Diana together with Queen Elizabeth II.

Others are full of frank advice for me and my family and some of them do not hesitate to be critical.

I value all these letters for keeping me in touch with your views and opinions, but there are a few letters which reflect the darker side of human nature.

It is only too easy for passionate loyalty to one's own country, race or religion, or even to one's favourite football club, to be corroded into intolerance, bigotry and ultimately into violence.

We have witnessed some frightening examples of this in recent years.

All too often intolerance creates the resentment and anger which fill the headlines and divide communities and nations and even families.

From time to time we also see some inspiring examples of tolerance.

Mr Gordon Wilson, whose daughter Marie lost her life in the horrifying explosion at Enniskillen on Remembrance Sunday, impressed the whole world by the depth of his forgiveness.

His strength, and that of his wife, and the courage of their daughter, came from their Christian conviction.

All of us will echo their prayer that out of the personal tragedies of Enniskillen may come a reconciliation between the communities.

There are striking illustrations of the way in which the many different religions can come together in peaceful harmony.

Each year I try to attend the Commonwealth Day interfaith Observance at Westminster Abbey. At that service all are united in their willingness to pray for the common good.

This is a symbol of mutual tolerance and I find it most encouraging. Of course it is right that people should hold their beliefs and their faiths strongly and sincerely, but perhaps we should also have the humility to accept that, while we each have a right to our own convictions, others have a right to theirs too.

I am afraid that the Christmas message of goodwill has usually evaporated by the time Boxing Day is over.

This year I hope we will continue to remember the many innocent victims of violence and intolerance and the suffering of their families. Christians are taught to love their neighbours, not just at Christmas, but all the year round.

I hope we will all help each other to have a happy Christmas and, when the New Year comes, resolve to work for tolerance and understanding between all people.

Happy Christmas to you all.

In the year just past, Prince Philip and I have joined in the celebrations of some notable anniversaries. The events which they marked were hundreds of years apart, but each was important enough to get much attention in 1988.

The earliest event which we remembered was the encounter with the Spanish Armada in 1588. The 400th anniversary fell in the same year in which we were able to mark the happy relations between Britain and Spain which now exist, by our state visit in Madrid.

Four hundred years after "the winds blew" and the Spanish ships were scattered, the events were remembered, without animosity, in both countries. This year, the present King of Spain showed me the rooms in the Escorial, where his predecessor, Philip the Second, planned the campaign. Had the fortunes of war gone against us, how very differently events in Britain and Europe would have unfolded.

Earlier in the year, we marked another event of the first importance in our history – the 300th anniversary of what is popularly known as the Glorious Revolution.

The invitation to King William and Queen Mary to accept the thrones of England and Scotland finally laid to rest the "enterprise of England" which Philip of Spain set in hand.

It thus gave the particular direction to our history which was to lead to the development of parliamentary democracy and the tradition of political and religious toleration which Britain enjoys today.

It was a great pleasure for us to celebrate that event in the company of the Crown Prince of The Netherlands. Together we visited Torbay – which was where King William landed in 1688.

It was shrouded with fog when we were there, but we did manage to see through the mist some of the hundreds of British and Dutch yachts that had assembled there.

The 1988 anniversary season opened in Australia – with a grand party on Australia Day to mark the country's 200th birthday. It was a party which went on for most of the year, but Prince Philip and I joined in the festivities in April and May.

Like so many visitors in bicentennial year we brought home some souvenirs of our visit. In our case it was some delightful early prints of Sydney, which served to remind us of the extraordinary developments which have taken place in Australia in the short space of 200 years.

The scenes of Sydney harbour contrast vividly with the pictures we all saw of the crowded waters around the opera house and the famous bridge in January this year. Centenaries may seem rather arbitrary occasions, but they nonetheless prompt us to look back into the past.

When we do so, we can draw hope from seeing how ancient enmities have vanished; and how new nations have grown and established themselves in vigour and wisdom.

Equally, they make us reflect on injustices and tragedies and inspire us to do our best to learn from these as well.

To do that, we surely should draw inspiration from one other anniversary – the one we celebrate every year at this time, the birth of Christ.

There are many grand and splendid pictures in the royal collection that illustrate this event, but one which gives me particular pleasure is a precious, almost jewel-like book.

It is a "Book of Hours", full of prayers and devotional readings. It's in Latin, but it contains the most exquisite illuminations and it is these that speak to us most movingly.

The anonymous person who drew the pictures nearly 500 years ago has included all the familiar elements of the Christmas story which we hear with such pleasure every year.

We find the angels, bringing the glad tidings to the shepherds, who listen attentively; the baby Jesus lies in his stall, with Mary and Joseph watching over him.

The star over the stable has lit the way for all of us ever since, and there should be no-one who feels shut out from that welcoming and guiding light.

The legends of Christmas about the ox and the ass suggest that even the animals are not outside that loving care.

Recently, many of you will have set up and decorated a Christmas tree in your homes. Often these are put by a window and the bright and shining tree is there for every passer-by to see and share.

I like to think that if someone who feels lonely and unloved should see such a tree, that person might feel "It was meant for me". May the Christmas story encourage you, for it is a message of hope every year, not for a few, but for all.

So in sending you my Christmas greeting, I pray that God may bless you – every one. As you probably all know, my Christmas broadcast has to be recorded well before Christmas Day so that it can be made available to radio and television stations throughout the Commonwealth.

Since I made that recording this year we have all been shocked and distressed by a series of major disasters – here in Britain, the worst air crash in our history at Lockerbie and a serious train accident at Clapham; and in Armenia a terrible earthquake.

All three came with great suddenness and destroyed the lives of many people who were looking forward to celebrating Christmas with their families and friends.

So, there are many homes today where the joy of Christmas has been darkened by a cloud of sadness and grief.

Our hearts and prayers go out to those who have been injured and bereaved and it is my hope that the eternal message of Christmas will bring some comfort in the hour of sadness.

World Events of 1988
* The Prince of Wales escaped death when an avalanche in Switzerland killed one of his friends.
* Artificial snow is needed to stage the Winter Olympics in Calgary.
* New licensing laws allow all day opening for British pubs.
* The Anglican Church in America appoints its first woman bishop.
* George Bush becomes US President.
* 'A Brief History of Time' by Dr Stephen Hawking is a best seller.
* Benazir Bhutto becomes Prime Minister of Pakistan.
* The Chilean dictator General Pinochet is defeated in elections.
* Pan Am flight 103 explodes and crashes on Lockerbie.
* Signal failure causes a rail disaster just outside Clapham Junction.

Sporting Life
* Fourth division Wimbledon win the English football FA Cup.
* Steffi Graf wins the "Grand Slam" and an Olympic gold medal.
* Nine athletes are disqualified from the Seoul Olympics after failing drugs tests.
* Florence Griffith-Joyner wins gold medals in the 100m and 200m.

The Arts
* Michael Jackson does a concert tour of the UK.
* Prince Charles attacks modern architects' English on TV.
* David Hockney staged a retrospective at the Tate in London.
* 'Acrobat and Young Harlequin' by Picasso sells for £20.9 million.
* Top films are 'Fatal Attraction' and 'A Fish Called Wanda'.

Top left:
At the Olympic Games in Seoul, South Korea, the Canadian sprinter Ben Johnson was stripped of his gold medal when a routine drugs test proved positive.

Below left:
On the night of the 21st December 1988 a Pan American Boeing jumbo jet crashed on and around the Scottish town of Lockerbie, in Dumfriesshire. All 259 people aboard Pan Am flight 103 together with 11 people on the ground were killed.

Left:
The American rock star Michael Jackson meets with Princess Diana during his world tour concert at Wembley Stadium, which was a spectacular success.

1989

World Events of 1989

- Ayatollah Khomeini orders the execution of British author Salman Rushdie.
- 95 football supporters, most from Liverpool die in the Hillsborough disaster.
- Chinese government troops open fire on demonstrators in Tiananmen Square.
- The Guildford Four were freed by the appeal court after they had served 14 years for a crime they did not commit.
- An earthquake causes massive destruction in San Francisco.
- Hungary becomes a republic and free elections are promised.
- The Berlin Wall opens at the Brandenburg Gate.
- Democratic revolution frees Czechoslovakia from communist rule.
- US and Soviet leaders declare an end to the Cold War.
- 10 days of civil war in Rumania end with the capture and execution of President Ceausescu and his wife.
- Proceedings in the House of Commons are televised for the first time.

Sporting Life

- Frank Bruno fails in his attempt to take the world heavyweight title from Mike Tyson.
- 'Desert Orchid' wins the Cheltenham Gold Cup.
- The jockey Peter Scudamore wins a record 200 races in one season.

The Arts

- Sean Connery stars with Harrison Ford in the new 'Indiana Jones' film.
- Remains of Shakespeare's Globe Theatre are found.
- Kenneth Branagh directs and stars in 'Henry V'.

Right:
Nations within the Soviet bloc were moving towards democracy and in China students and workers were demonstrating against corruption and for political reforms. Over 1 million gathered each day in Tiananmen Square. Deng Xiaoping ordered a crackdown, and possibly 1,000 people were killed.

Left:
Major Dick Hern, flat horseracing trainer. is introduced to Queen Elizabeth II prior to being presented by her with the cup after winning the King George and Queen Elizabeth Diamond Stakes with Nashwan.

This year I thought I would speak particularly to the children of the Commonwealth.

All parents would like their children to grow up in peace and tranquillity, but for most of this century the people of this world have had to live through bewildering changes and upheavals.

Some of the changes have been for the better, but others might even threaten the world we live in. There are some children who are much less fortunate than others, for they come from countries where nature makes life very hard, with floods and droughts and other disasters destroying crops, making it very difficult to find enough for everyone to eat.

Quite a lot of you have written to me during the last year or so, saying how worried you are about the future of our planet.

Many of you will have heard of the greenhouse effect, and perhaps you've heard, too, about even more urgent problems caused by the pollution of our rivers and seas and the cutting down of the great forests.

These problems don't affect just the countries where they are happening and they make neighbouring co-operation throughout the world a pressing necessity.

With all your lives before you, I am sure that you take an optimistic view of the future. But it is already too late to prevent all forms of damage to the natural world.

Some species of wild plants and animals are, sadly, bound to become extinct. But the great thing to remember is that it is not too late to reduce the damage if we change our attitudes and behaviour.

You've all seen pictures of the Earth taken from space. Unlike all the other planets in the solar system, Earth shimmers green and blue in the sunlight and looks a very pleasant place to live.

These pictures should remind us that the future of all life on Earth depends on how we behave towards one another, and how we treat the plants and animals that share our world with us.

Men and women have shown themselves to be very clever at inventing things, right back to the time when they found out how much easier it was to move things about on wheels, up to the present time when rockets and computers make it possible for people to travel away from our world out into the mystery of space.

But these technical skills are not enough by themselves. They can only come to the rescue of the planet if we also learn to live by the golden rule which Jesus Christ taught us – "Love thy neighbour as thyself".

Many of you will have heard the story of the Good Samaritan, and of how Christ answered the question (from a clever lawyer who was trying to catch him out) "Who is my neighbour?" Jesus told of the traveller who was mugged and left injured on the roadside where several important people saw him, and passed by without stopping to help.

His neighbour was the man who did stop, cared for him, and made sure he was being well looked after before he resumed his own journey.

It's not very difficult to apply that story to our own times and to work out that our neighbours are those of our friends, or complete strangers, who need a helping hand.

Do you think they might also be some of the living species threatened by spoiled rivers, or some of the children in places like Ethiopia and Sudan who don't have enough to eat?

The exciting news of the last few months has been the way in which people in both East and West Europe have begun to think about the future in a less unfriendly way – more as neighbours.

It's still hard for us to be sure what is going to happen as a result of these great events, but it would be splendid to think that in the last years of the 20th century Christ's message about loving our neighbours as ourselves might at last be heeded.

If it is, they'll be good years for you to grow up in. If we can reduce selfishness and jealousy, dishonesty and injustice, the nineties can become a time of peace and tranquillity for children and grown-ups, and a time for working together for the benefit of our planet as a whole.

You children have something to give us which is priceless. You can still look at the world with a sense of wonder and remind us grown-ups that life is wonderful and precious. Often a child's helplessness and vulnerability bring out the best in us.

Part of that "best" in us could be a particular tenderness towards this Earth which we share as human beings, all of us, and, together, as the nations of the world, will leave to our children and our children's children. We must be kind to it for their sake.

In the hope that we will be kind and loving to one another, not just on Christmas Day, but throughout the year,

I wish you all a very happy Christmas. God bless you.

Over the years, I have dwelt on the happier side of life in my Christmas broadcasts – we need reminding of it, particularly at Christmas time. This year, there have been, I hope, times of happiness and good cheer for most of us.

My family, for instance, has been celebrating my mother's 90th birthday, and we have shared with you the joy of some of those celebrations. My youngest grandchild's christening, two days ago, has brought the family together once again. I hope that all of us lucky enough to be able to enjoy such gatherings this Christmas will take time to count our blessings.

For it seems to me that there is one deep and overriding anxiety for us all on which we should reflect today. That is the threat of war in the Middle East. The servicemen in the Gulf who are spending Christmas at their posts under this threat are much in our thoughts. And there are many others, at home and abroad, servicemen and civilians, who are away from their own firesides. Wherever they are, may they all, when their duty is done, soon be reunited with their families safe and sound.

At the same time we must remember those still held hostage. Some of them have spent years in captivity and Christmas must for them be especially hard to bear. My heart goes out to them and to their families. We can, at least, rejoice at the safe return of many of their compatriots over the last weeks, and salute the courage which they have shown.

Wars, threats of wars and civil disturbance inevitably cause thousands of innocent people to become refugees and to have their lives ruined or disrupted. It is difficult for us, safe at home, to contemplate the scale of the suffering for homeless and hungry people caused by the ever-widening consequences of the crisis in the Gulf.

The invasion of Kuwait was an example on an international scale of an evil which has beset us at different levels in recent years – attempts by ruthless people to impose their will on the peaceable majority. In extreme form, as we know only too well, these attempts lead to disaster and death, and their tragic aftermath for families and communities. In the United Kingdom, we have suffered once again during the past year from the scourge of terrorism, its disregard for human life and its efforts to dress its crimes in political clothes.

But all this is nothing new. The tributes we paid last summer to the heroes of Dunkirk and the Battle of Britain were tributes to their achievement in repelling a determined invader. That was 50 years ago.

Nowadays there are all too many causes that press their claims with a loud voice and a strong arm rather than with the language of reason. We must not allow ourselves to be too discouraged as we confront them. Let us remember that Christ did not promise the earth to the powerful. The resolve of those who endure and resist these activities should not be underestimated.

I never cease to admire the stoical courage of those in Northern Ireland, for example, who go about their business in defiance of the terrorist. The reaction of those who have lost loved ones at violent hands is often an inspiration to the rest of us. Then again, I, like many others, was much heartened by the virtually unanimous opposition of the international community to the unprovoked invasion of Kuwait, and by the speed with which moves were made to try to relieve the plight of the innocent victims.

I want, therefore, to say thank you today to the men and women who, day in and day out, carry on their daily life in difficult and dangerous circumstances. By just getting on with the job, they are getting the better of those who want to harm our way of life. Let us think of them this Christmas, wherever they are in the world, and pray that their resolution remains undiminished. It is they and their kind who, by resisting the bully and the tyrant, ensure that we live in the sort of world in which we can celebrate this season safely with our families.

I pray also that we may all be blessed with something of their spirit. Then we would find it easier to solve our disputes in peace and justice, wherever they occur, and that inheritance of the earth which Christ promised, not to the strong, but to the meek, would be that much closer.

A happy Christmas and God bless you all.

Right:
State visit of President Cossiga of Italy in October 1990 together with Prince Philip, and Queen Elizabeth II.

1990

World Events of 1990
* Nelson Mandela is freed from prison.
* A protest march against the Poll Tax in London turns into a riot.
* France bans British beef imports amid concern over BSE.
* Two English teenage girls are arrested in Bangkok in possession of heroin.
* Irish hostage Brian Keenan is released from Beirut.
* Saddam Hussein invades Kuwait and detains hundreds of foreigners in Baghdad.
* Lech Walesa wins a victory in presidential elections in Poland.
* John Major ousts Margaret Thatcher in a party election to become Prime Minister.
* French and English tunnellers meet under the Channel.
* Benazir Bhutto is sacked as Prime Minister of Pakistan.

Sporting Life
* Martina Navratilova wins a record ninth ladies singles title at Wimbledon.
* West Germany wins football's World Cup in Rome.
* Stephen Hendry becomes the youngest ever world snooker champion.

The Arts
* The opera highlight is the Three Tenors at the World Cup in Rome.
* Financial problems close the Barbican and the Royal Opera House.
* 'Ghost' and 'Cyrano de Bergerac' are hit films.
* Julia Roberts, starring in 'Pretty Woman' and 'Sleeping with the Enemy', is this years top female actress.
* Arnold Schwarzenegger is this years most popular male star with roles in 'Kindergarten Cop' and 'Total Recall'.
* The Simpsons make their first airing on TV, and Bart Simpson immediately becomes every teenager's hero.
* 'Home Alone' turns boy star Macaulay Culkin into a household name, as he outwits a duo of burglars.
* Teenage Mutant Ninja Turtles is the other unlikely success story of the year.

Left:
In South Africa Nelson Mandela was sentenced to life imprisonment in 1964 for his anti-government activities. After his release in February 1990 he became leader of the ANC and negotiated a peaceful transition to multiracial democracy.

* US athlete Mike Powell breaks the long jump record at the world championships.
* England's rugby union team wins the Five Nations championship.
* Manchester United win the European Cup-Winners Cup.

Top left:
Infrantry Soldiers of the British 4th Armoured Brigade fight deep inside Iraq territory during the Gulf War as Operation 'Desert Storm' gets underway.

Centre:
Hostage Terry Waite, on his release from captivity.

Left:
Luciano Pavarotti performing to raptured crowds in a free concert at Hyde Park.

World Events of 1991
* Operation "Desert Storm" against Iraq begins.
* Saddam Hussein releases oil into the Gulf.
* The Gulf War ends after six weeks.
* The "Birmingham Six" are freed by an appeal court.
* Rajiv Gandhi is killed.
* Helen Sharman is Britain's first astronaut.
* Winnie Mandela is sentenced to six years in prison.
* Gorbachev collects the Nobel peace prize, and is toppled by communists.
* John McCarthy and later Terry Waite are released from captivity in Lebanon.
* A mortar lands in the garden of 10 Downing Street.
* The poll tax is abandoned.
* A new famine hits Africa.
* Yugoslavia drifts towards civil war.
* The Maxwell empire collapses after Peter Maxwell's mysterious death.

* President Bush and Gorbachev sign a ground breaking nuclear arms reduction treaty and subsequently cut nuclear weapons stockpiles.

Sporting Life
* Michael Jordan, America's top basket-ball player and sporting personality announces retirement due to the fact that he has tested HIV-positive.
* South Africa admitted to international sport after a 21-year boycott campaign.

The Arts
* Pavarotti sings at a free concert in Hyde Park.
* 'I do it for you' by Bryan Adams tops the UK charts for a record 16 weeks.
* On English television, David Jason stars in 'The Darling Buds of May'.
* Mozart features heavily in his bicentennial year.
* 'Silence of the Lambs' wins five Oscars.
* Kevin Costner, star of 'Robin Hood: Prince of Thieves' and 'JFK', was the most popular male box-office attraction of the year.
* Michael Jackson becomes the world's highest paid recording artist with his one billion dollar multimedia deal with Sony.
* Sega's new Sonic the Hedgehog game sets new world records.
* Nirvana and lead singer Curt Cobain are the new idols of pop, and front the "grunge" movement.

In 1952, when I first broadcast to you at Christmas, the world was a very different place to the one we live in today. Only seven years had passed since the end of one of the most destructive wars in the history of mankind. Even the end of hostilities didn't bring the true peace for which so many had fought and died.

What became known as the cold war sustained an atmosphere of suspicion, anxiety and fear for many years. Then, quite suddenly, everything began to change, and the changes have happened with bewildering speed. In 1989 the Berlin wall came down. Since then the rest of the world has watched fascinated as oppressive regimes have crumbled under popular pressure. One by one these liberated peoples have taken the first hesitant and sometimes painful steps towards open and democratic society.

Naturally, we welcome this, and it may be that we can help them achieve their aims. But in doing that, we need to remind ourselves of the elements which form the bedrock of our own free way of life – so highly valued and so easily taken for granted. This can be an opportunity to reflect on our good fortune, and on whether we have anything to offer by way of example to those who have recently broken free of dictatorship. We, who claim to be of the free world, should examine what we mean by freedom, and how we can help to ensure that, once in place, it is there to stay.

There are all sorts of elements to a free society but I believe that among the most important is the willingness of ordinary men and women to play a part in the life of their community rather than confining themselves to their own narrow interests. The part they play may not be a major one, indeed they can frequently turn out to be thankless tasks. The wonder is, though, that there are so many who are prepared to devote much of their lives with no reward to their fellow men and women.

Without their dedication, where would our churches or charities be, for instance? Without such people many would be unable to enjoy the pleasure that the arts bring to our daily lives. Governments can encourage and support but it is the volunteers who work away for nothing in administration or spend their weekends seeing fair play that make sport and physical recreation so worthwhile. I am constantly amazed by the generosity of donors and subscribers, great and small, who give so willingly and often towards the enjoyment of others. Without them, these voluntary organisations simply would not exist.

The peoples of the former Soviet Union and Eastern Europe have broken the mould of autocracy. I hope that we will be able to help them as they learn that the democracy which has replaced it depends, not on political structures, but on the goodwill and the sense of responsibility of each and every citizen.

It is not, of course, as simple as that. All the selfless voluntary work in the world can be wasted if it disregards the views and aspirations of others. There are any number of reasons to find fault with each other, with our governments, and with other countries. But let us not take ourselves too seriously. None of us has a monopoly of wisdom and we must always be ready to listen to and respect other points of view.

At the Commonwealth heads of government meeting in Zimbabwe this autumn we saw an example of mutual tolerance and respect for the views of others on an international scale. The leaders of 50 nations came together to discuss the future. They met in peace, they talked freely, they listened, they found much on which to agree, and they set a new direction for the Commonwealth. I am sure that each derived strength and reassurance in the process.

That was just one event in a year of massive and historic change. This time last year we were thinking of the servicemen and women in the Gulf, and of the hostages in captivity. Our prayers for their safe homecoming have largely been answered. This Christmas we can take heart in seeing how, in the former Soviet Union and Eastern Europe, where it has endured years of persecution and hardship, the Christian faith is once again thriving and able to spread its message of unselfishness, compassion and tolerance.

Next February will see the fortieth anniversary of my father's death and of my accession. Over the years I have tried to follow my father's example and to serve you as best I can. You have given me, in return, your loyalty and your understanding, and for that I give you my heartfelt thanks. I feel the same obligation to you that I felt in 1952. With your prayers, and your help, and with the love and support of my family, I shall try to serve you in the years to come.

May God bless you and bring you a happy Christmas.

1992

Top:
In March former heavyweight boxing champion Mike Tyson is fined $30,000 and sentenced to six years in prison on rape charges by an Indianapolis court.

Far right and below:
Queen Elizabeth celebrated her 40th anniversary as sovereign but the media attention surrounding her children's marriage difficulties, added to the disaster of the fire at Windsor Castle made 1992 her "annus horribilus".

World Events of 1992

* The West sends food and medical aid to Russia.
* The Yugoslav confederation is broken up.
* The UK suffers its worst drought since 1745.
* Mike Tyson gets a six-year jail sentence for rape.

* Andrew Morton publishes 'Diana: Her True Story'.
* The Bishop of Galway resigns after revelations that he has an illegitimate son.
* Anti-Mafia judge Falcone is murdered in Sicily.
* 58 die in race riots in Los Angeles.
* The Duchess of York announces that she is seeking a divorce, and the Prince and Princess of Wales separate.
* Windsor Castle is badly damaged by fire.
* Chris Patten becomes the last Governor of Hong Kong.

Sporting Life

* Pakistan beat England by 22 runs to win the World Cup in Melbourne.
* David Platt is sold to Italian club Juventus for £8 million.
* Nigel Mansell becomes the Formula One world champion.
* The "Unified Team" of former Soviet Union athletes scooped 112 Olympic medals.

The Arts

* Kenneth Branagh played 'Hamlet'.
* Paul McCartney's 'Oratorio' was premiered.
* Emma Thompson wins an Oscar for her role in 'Howard's End'.

This year I am speaking to you not from Buckingham Palace, but from Sandringham where my family gathers every year for Christmas. My great-grandfather, King Edward VII made Sandringham his country home in 1862 and it was from this house that my grandfather, King George V, and my father used to speak over the radio – originally to the Empire and then to the Commonwealth – on Christmas Day all those years ago.

It was from here that I made my first Christmas broadcast 40 years ago and this year I am very glad to be able to speak to you again from this family home. I first came here for Christmas as a grandchild. Nowadays my grandchildren come here for the same family festival. To me this continuity is a great source of comfort in a world of tension and violence.

The peace and tranquillity of the Norfolk countryside make me realise how fortunate we are and all the more conscious of the trials and sorrows that so many people are suffering both in this country and around the world. My heart goes out to those whose lives have been blighted by war, terrorism, famine, natural disaster or economic hardship.

Like many other families, we have lived through some difficult days this year. The prayers, understanding and sympathy given to us by so many of you, in good times and bad, have lent us great support and encouragement. It has touched me deeply that much of this has come from those of you who have troubles of your own.

As some of you may have heard me observe, it has, indeed, been a sombre year. But Christmas is surely the right moment to try to put it behind us and find a moment to pray for those, wherever they are, who are doing their best in all sorts of ways to make things better in 1993. I am thinking especially of the servicemen and women, and the aid workers with them, trying to keep the peace in countries riven by strife and to bring food to the weak and innocent victims. They do not have an easy task and they need all the moral and practical support we can give them.
Curiously enough, it was a sad event which did as much as anything in 1992 to help me put my own worries into perspective. Just before he died, Leonard Cheshire came to see us with his fellow members of the Order of Merit. By then he was suffering from a long drawn-out and terminal illness. He bore this with all the fortitude and cheerfulness to be expected of a holder of the Victoria Cross.

However, what struck me more forcibly than his physical courage was the fact that he made no reference to his own illness, but only to his hopes and plans to make life better for others. He embodied the message in those well-known lines: "Kindness is another's trouble, courage is one's own."

One of his Cheshire Homes for people with disabilities is not far from this house. I have visited others all over the Commonwealth and I have seen at first hand the remarkable results of his and his wife's determination to put Christ's teaching to practical effect. Perhaps this shining example of what a human being can achieve in a lifetime of dedication can inspire in the rest of us a belief in our own capacity to help others.

Such talents and indomitable spirit are not given to all of us. But if we can sometimes lift our eyes from our own problems and focus on those of others, it will be at least a step in the right direction and Christmas is a good time to take it.
1993 will certainly bring new challenges, but let us resolve to meet it with fresh hope in our hearts. There is no magic formula that will transform sorrow into happiness, intolerance into compassion, or war into peace. But inspiration can change human behaviour. Those like Leonard Cheshire, who devote their lives to others, have that inspiration and they know and we know where to look for help in finding it. That help can be readily given if we only have their faith to ask. I and my family, as we approach a new year, will draw strength from this faith in our commitment to your service in the coming years. I pray that each and every one of you has a happy Christmas and that we can all try to bring that happiness to others. God bless you all.

Four generations of my family have enjoyed the quiet and solitude of this library. It is still a haven of peace even if my grandchildren do their best over Christmas to make it rather more lively!

Most of the books on the shelves date from my great-grandfather's time and their titles reflect the life and events of those days.

Books are one of the ways in which each generation can communicate its history, values and culture to the next. There are books here about the statesmen, explorers, warriors and saints; there are many about war, especially the First World War, which ended 75 years ago. Families and loved ones of those who fought in it knew little of the horrors of the trenches, other than from artists' drawings or photographs such as these – often published days or weeks after the event. Nowadays stories and pictures from all over the world can be gathered up and appear in print within hours.

We have indeed become a global village. It is no longer possible to plead ignorance about what is going on in far-off parts of the world. Switch on the radio or television and the graphic details of distant events are instantly available to us. Not all the pictures bring gloomy news. This year has seen significant progress made towards solving some of the world's most difficult problems – the Middle East, for instance, the democratic future of South Africa, and, most recently, Northern Ireland.

All too often, though, we find ourselves watching or listening to the sort of news which, as a daily diet, can be almost overwhelming. It makes us yearn for some good news.

If we can look on the bright side, so much the better, but that does not mean we should shield ourselves from the truth, even if it is unwelcome. I believe that we should be aware of events which, in the old days, might have passed us by. But that means facing up to the question of what we can do to use that awareness for the greater good.

The simple answer is, of course, all too little. But there is another answer. It is that the more we know, the more we feel responsible, and the more we want to help. Those involved in international charity work confirm that modern communications have helped to bring them public support and made them more effective. People are not shunning the added responsibility, but shouldering it.

All of us owe a debt to those volunteers who are out there in the front line, putting our donations to use by looking after the wounded, the hungry and the oppressed. Much of their work never reaches the headlines or television screens, but their example should inspire us all the same. We cannot all follow them the whole way, but we can do something to help within our own community – particularly at Christmas, when those without work or the company of family or friends feel especially left out.

I am always moved by those words in St John's Gospel which we hear on Christmas Day: "He was in the world, and the world was made by him, and the world knew him not". We have only to listen to the news to know the truth of that. But the Gospel goes on: "But as many as received him, to them gave he power to become the sons of God." For all the inhumanity around us, let us be grateful for those who have received him and who go about quietly doing their work and his will without thought of reward or recognition. They know that there is an eternal truth of much greater significance than our own triumphs and tragedies, and it is embodied by the child in the manger. This is their message of hope.

We can all try to reflect that message of hope in our own lives, in our actions and in our prayers. If we do, the reflection may light the way for others and help them to read the message too. We live in the global village, but villages are made up of families. We, the peoples of the 50 nations of the Commonwealth – more than a quarter of the world's population – have, as members of one of the largest families, a great responsibility. By working together, we can help the rest of the world become a more humane and happier place.

I am reminded this year of some lines from a Christmas hymn which many of you will know:

"Yet in thy dark streets shineth
The everlasting Light –
The hopes and fears of all the years
Are met in thee tonight."

In Northern Ireland especially, these last years, fear has made the streets dark indeed. Now we have seen that the light of hope can brighten them. May 1994 bring to those brave people who live there and go about their lawful lives undaunted, the reward they deserve – peace.

I hope you all enjoy your Christmas. I pray, with you, for a happy and peaceful New Year.

Right:
Queen Elizabeth II with the Queen Mother and Princess Anne.

1993

World Events of 1993
* Two ten-year-olds are charged with the murder of James Bulger.
* The Queen volunteers to pay tax on her private income.
* Bill Clinton becomes President of the USA.
* Yitzhak Rabin and Yasser Arafat shake hands on the White House lawn.
* Former Philippines first lady Imelda Marcos is sentenced to 18 years in prison for corruption.
* Benazir Bhutto returns to power in Pakistan.
* President Yeltsin crushes a rebellion in Moscow.
* Australia restores lands to the Aborigines.
* Ffyona Campbell completes a 10,000-mile walk across Africa.
* Stella Rimington, head of MI5, reveals details of the work of her organisation.

Sporting Life
* Demonstrations bring chaos to the Grand National.
* Tennis star Monica Seles is stabbed during a match.
* Pete Sampras wins the Wimbledon men's singles championship.
* Brazil's Ayrton Senna wins the last Formula One race of the season in Adelaide.

The Arts
* Eric Clapton wins six Grammy awards.
* Top film stars call for an end to screen violence.
* Spielberg's 'Jurassic Park' cost a reported £68 million to make.
* Rachel Whiteread wins the Turner prize for 'Untitled Room'.
* Salman Rushdie wins the "Booker of Bookers" prize for 'Midnight's Children'.

Top left:
US tennis player Pete Sampras celebrates a win which led to his winning the Wimbledon men's singles championship.

Below left:
'Untitled Room' by Rachel Whiteread – a giant-sized sculpture in a London Street.

Below left:
Top film director, Steven Spielberg's blockbuster movie 'Jurassic Park' is launched and grosses over $500 million in box office takings worldwide during 1993.

1994

World Events of 1994

A major earthquake hits Los Angeles.
Lieutenant-General Sir Michael Rose is appointed to lead a UN peace-keeping force in Bosnia.
Priests and bishops leave the Church of England in protest at women's ordination.
Frederick and Rosemary West are charged with murder when eight bodies are discovered buried at their home in Gloucester.
Tony Blair is elected leader of the Labour Party after John Smith's death in May.
O. J. Simpson is arrested.

The terrorist, Carlos the Jackal, is finally captured.
The ferry 'Estonia' with over 1,000 passengers on board sinks in the Baltic.

Veterans mark the 50th anniversary of the D-Day landings.
An estimated 100,000 are killed in tribal slaughter in Rwanda.

Sporting Life

Ayrton Senna dies in a crash at the San Marino Grand Prix.
Brazil wins the World Cup for the fourth time.
Torvill and Dean win the British Ice Dancing championship scoring nine sixes.
Spanish cyclist Miguel Indurain wins the Tour de France.
Diane Modahl gets a four-year ban after failing drug tests.

The Arts

'Four Weddings and a Funeral' is a hit film.
Steven Spielberg's 'Schindler's List' wins seven Oscars.
The "Three Graces" sculpture by Canova is to remain in Britain.

Left:
Veterans of the Second World War gathered on the beaches of Normandy to mark the 50th anniversary of the D-Day landings.

Left inset:
Former American football star O.J. Simpson was arrested and charged in June with the murder of his ex-wife, Nicole, and a male companion.

Below left:
The British Labour Party in opposition in 1994 elected Tony Blair as their new leader. Labour went on to win a landslide victory against the Conservatives in May 1997.

I shall never forget the events in Normandy last June, when the representatives of the wartime allies commemorated the 50th anniversary of the D-Day landings. We who were there, and millions of others through television and radio, paid fitting tribute to the courage of those who took part in that epic campaign.

As Prince Philip and I stood watching the British veterans march past on the beach at Arromanches, my own memories of 1944 were stirred – of how it was to wait anxiously for news of friends and relations engaged in that massive and hazardous operation; of the subsequent ebb and flow of the battles in France and then in Germany itself, and of the gradual realisation that the war really was at last coming to an end.

Since those D-Day commemorations, Prince Philip and I have been to Russia. While we were in St Petersburg, we had the opportunity to honour the millions of patriotic Russians who died fighting the common enemy. To see British and Russian veterans standing together, in memory of the sacrifices of their comrades-in-arms, was a moving experience. I never thought it would be possible in my lifetime to join with the Patriarch of Moscow and his congregation in a service in that wonderful cathedral in the heart of the Moscow Kremlin.

This Christmas, as we pray for peace at home and abroad – not least in Russia itself – we can also give thanks that such cathedrals and churches will be full and that the great bells, which greeted us, will be ringing out to celebrate our Saviour's birth.

We are frequently reminded, of course, that violence and hatred are still all too much in evidence. We can take some comfort, however, from the fact that more people throughout the world, year by year, have real hope of their children growing up in peace and free from fear.

Last Christmas we were witnessing the signs of a new dawn after the long night of bitterness, and this year these signs have become steadily stronger. If that new dawn is to be a real, and not a false one, courage, patience and faith will be sorely needed – those same qualities which kept the flame of hope alive in the war-torn countries of Europe and the Far East in the dark days of the last war.

Christ taught us to love our enemies and to do good to them that hate us. It is a hard lesson to learn, but this year we have seen shining examples of that generosity of spirit which alone can banish division and prejudice. In Northern Ireland, peace is gradually taking root; a fully democratic South Africa has been welcomed back into the Commonwealth; and, in the Middle East, long standing enmities are healing.

What is it that makes people turn from violence, and try to bring peace to their community? Most of all, I believe, it is their determination to bring reality to their hopes of a better world for their children.

The sight of the happy faces of children and young people in Russia, in South Africa, where so much has changed with such extraordinary speed in the last year, and in Northern Ireland, where there is real hope of a permanent end to the bitterness of recent years, should be enough to convince even the most hard-hearted that peace is worth striving for.

Next year, we shall commemorate the 50th anniversary of the end of the Second World War. The celebrations will no doubt be spectacular, and I hope we all enjoy them. But we can also, each in our own way, ensure that they leave a lasting mark in history. If we resolve to be considerate and to help our neighbours; to make friends with people of different races and religions; and, as our Lord said, to look to our own faults before we criticise others, we will be keeping faith with those who landed in Normandy and fought so doggedly for their belief in freedom, peace and human decency.

The poet Siegfried Sassoon, amidst all the horrors of war, still found himself able to write these words: "Everyone's voice was suddenly lifted / And beauty came like the setting sun".

If he could see the beauty from the trenches of Flanders, surely we can look for it in our own lives, this Christmas and in the coming year.

Happy Christmas and God bless you.

Right:
Queen Elizabeth II meets war veterans in France during the celebrations of the 50th Anniversary of D-Day

1995

World Events of 1995
* Kobe, a city in Japan, is devastated by an earthquake.
* Michael Foale becomes the first Briton to walk in space.
* Nick Leeson bankrupts Barings Bank.
* A religious sect is responsible for a gas attack on the Tokyo underground system.
* Sinn Fein leader Gerry Adams is welcomed at a White House party.
* Timothy McVeigh bombs the Oklahoma City's federal building.
* The first DNA database opens in Birmingham.
* Winnie Mandela is dismissed from the South African government.
* A UN women's conference is held in Beijing.
* Japan apologises for their actions during the Pacific War on the 50th anniversary of its ending.
* O. J. Simpson is acquitted.
* The world population is 5.7 billion.

Below:
O.J.Simpson
American actor
and former athlete
is acquitted.

Above: On April 19th a truck filled with 4,000 pounds of explosive exploded in front of the Alfred P. Murrah Federal Building, Oklaholma City, 168 people were killed, including 12 children.

Below: In June South Africa beat New Zealand 15 – 12, the win was celebrated joyfully in South Africa as a momentary relief in turbulent times.

Sporting Life
* 40 – 1 outsider 'Royal Athlete' wins the Grand National.
* South Africa wins the Rugby Union World Cup.
* Steffi Graf wins Wimbledon, the US Open and the French Open.

The Arts
* Rock band 'Blur' wins four Brit Awards.
* Oscar Wilde is admitted to Poets' Corner in Westminster Abbey.
* 'Braveheart' wins the Oscar for best film.

In 1995 the nation and the Commonwealth have been celebrating the anniversary of VE-Day and VJ-Day. In quieter moments we also remembered those who paid the price for our freedom.

Commemorations and anniversaries are very important elements in our national life. Last summer we paid tribute, 50 years on, to all those who took part in the deadly events of the Second World War. In May we gave thanks for the end of the war in Europe, and then in August, for the first time since the end of the war in the Far East, we gave a real welcome home to the veterans of Burma and the Pacific.

It was difficult to know that day who felt the greater pride, those of us watching or those on parade. It was an unforgettable day for all of us.

The war demanded immense sacrifices and acts of selfless endurance and bravery but the final victory gave much of the world 50 years of relative peace. All generations since then have had good reason to be grateful to those who gave their service and, in all too many cases, their health or their lives, so that the rest of us could enjoy the freedom to get on with our lives in peace.

The work for peace is never-ending. At long last the fighting between the factions in the former Yugoslavia seems to be coming to an end, with life beginning to return to some kind of normality. This Christmas, thousands of Commonwealth servicemen and women will be far from their families, already playing their part in the international force dedicated to keeping that peace.

Closer to home, there has been a peace in Northern Ireland for more than a year. It is heartily welcomed by all people of goodwill. These are the first fruits of that ceaseless work for peace. They could only have been achieved by the quiet and determined efforts of all sorts of different people, some of them famous, many of them unnoticed and unsung by the world at large, but all peacemakers nonetheless. It is when the fighting ceases that the work of reconciliation and reconstruction can begin.

A short time ago, I invited a number of workers from volunteer organisations to Buckingham Palace. They came from all over the Commonwealth and they had worked in many countries, from Bosnia to Rwanda, from Chechnya to Cambodia. They go quietly about their business, in harrowing and dangerous circumstances, giving help to the suffering and the hungry.

Like the people who fought and won the last war, they make no claim to be anything out of the ordinary but their commitment is very far from ordinary. And their contribution is something of which all their compatriots can feel deeply proud.

It was during my visit to South Africa last March that I witnessed a glowing example of how the inspiration and energy of one person can benefit thousands of others.

Seven years ago, Sister Ethel came to a township outside Port Elizabeth where she began teaching young children under the shade of a solitary tree. Through her hard work and tenacity she has now built a pre-school and a clinic. These provide for children and teenagers who have missed out on formal education.

Soup and bread are distributed to the heads of 500 families from the township each day and, through the gift of a piece of waste ground by the local council, people are being taught to cultivate the land and grow their own vegetables. But I suspect that Sister Ethel's modesty and sense of humour prevent her from appreciating the full extent of her achievements.

The traditional Christmas message speaks of peace and goodwill among men. It is the volunteers and the Sister Ethels of this world who spread that message and it is for the rest of us to welcome it.

Christ said: "Blessed are the peacemakers, for they shall be called the children of God." Thanks to the peacemakers, many millions will enjoy a better Christmas this year. I hope your Christmas will be a happy one. God bless you all.

Left:
Queen Elizabeth II meets war veterans during VJ Day celebrations in London.

World Events of 1996

* Hillary Clinton testifies before a grand jury investigating the Whitewater affair.
* French ex-President François Mitterand dies after a long illness.
* Diana agrees to Prince Charles' request for a divorce.
* A teacher and 16 children are killed by a gunman at Dunblane.
* British beef exports are banned because of fears of "mad cow disease".
* Kevin and Ian Maxwell are cleared of charges of defrauding the Maxwell empire's pension funds.
* Yeltsin becomes President of Russia.
* NASA scientists say they have found evidence of possible life on Mars.
* A bomb explodes during the Olympic Games in Atlanta.
* Russian troops withdraw from Chechenya.
* Taliban militia in Afghanistan capture Kabul.

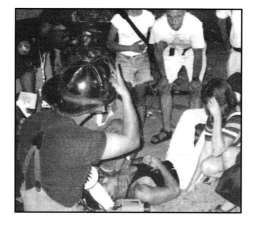

Above: On July 27th a bomb explodes in the Centennial Olympic Park during a rock concert, two people die and 111 are injured.

Left: Beef cattle in the UK were slaughtered and incinerated when it was discovered that BSE in cattle had spread to humans. The disease was spread as a result of feeding infected animal products to cattle.

Sporting Life

* England wins the Rugby Union Five Nations trophy.
* Carl Lewis takes the Olympic gold medal for long jump for the fourth time running.
* Bjarne Riis of Denmark wins the Tour de France.
* Krajicek wins the first Wimbledon men's final to be played between two unseeded players.
* Donovan Bailey sets a world record of 9.84 secs for the 100 metres.

The Arts

* 'The English Patient' wins an Oscar for best film.
* Oasis dominates the British pop scene.
* The Scottish film 'Trainspotting' is a surprise hit in the USA and Britain.
* The Lyric Opera of Chicago stages Wagner's 'The Ring' in a performance lasting 15 hours.

Above: Prior to their separation in 1992 the tension between the royal couple was self evident.

To look back is not necessarily to be nostalgic. When I come to Sandringham each year, I like to reflect on what Christmas must have been like when King Edward VII, my great-grandfather, and Queen Alexandra first came here as young parents. I remember my own childhood Christmases here, with my father and mother, and a great family gathering, and now I delight in seeing my children and grandchildren enjoying the same traditions.

Christmas is the celebration of the birth of the founder of the Christian faith, an event which took place almost 2000 years ago; every year, at this time, we are asked to look back at that extraordinary story and remind ourselves of the message which inspired Christ's followers then, and which is just as relevant today.

At Christmas I enjoy looking back on some of the events of the year. Many have their roots in history but still have a real point for us today. I recall, especially, a dazzling spring day in Norwich when I attended the Maundy Service, the cathedral providing a spectacular setting. The lovely service is always a reminder of Christ's words to His disciples: "Love one another, as I have loved you." It sounds so simple, yet it proves so hard to obey.

In June came Trooping the Colour, a vivid reminder of this country's proud military tradition and of the discipline and dedication which our servicemen and women show in their taxing tasks of peace-keeping in many distant parts of the world.

Then, in October, I opened Parliament. This is not just a state occasion but is also symbolic of the process of parliamentary democracy which we enjoy here in Britain and in so many countries of the Commonwealth. It is a process which seeks to express the ideal of the equality of all citizens under the law.

So, the past, with its traditions, has its lessons for us in 1996. This year, in our travels, Prince Philip and I have also been looking to the future. I and all my family have always felt that one of our most important duties is to express, in our visits overseas, the goodwill of our country towards friends abroad, near and far.

So, last spring, we visited Poland and the Czech Republic, where we saw the development of democracy and prosperity in countries which only recently were communist-governed. And everywhere we received the best of welcomes.

In the autumn we went to Thailand, where we renewed old friendships and witnessed the blending of tradition with a dynamic commercial spirit.

There was also a happy visit to this country by the President of France. And I shall never forget the state visit of President Mandela. That most gracious of men has shown us all how to accept the facts of the past without bitterness, how to see new opportunities as more important than old disputes and how to look forward with courage and optimism. His example is a continuing inspiration to the whole Commonwealth and to all those everywhere who work for peace and reconciliation.

Each year brings its share of difficulties for many families. This year has, I know, been no exception. And during it some have suffered bereavement of a tragic and shocking kind. At such times, it is tempting for all of us, especially those who suffer, to look back and say "If only". But to look back in that way is to look down a blind alley. Better to look forward and say "If only". If only we can live up to the example of the child who was born at Christmas with a love that came to embrace the whole world.

If only we can let Him recapture for us that time when we face the future with childhood's unbounded faith. Armed with that faith, the new year, with all its challenges and chances, should hold no terrors for us, and we should be able to embark upon it undaunted.

My family joins me in wishing each one of you a very happy Christmas.

Far right:
Queen Elizabeth II outside St Paul's Cathedral. The Queen unveiled a memorial to the 47 British servicemen who died in the Gulf War.

Right:
Queen Elizabeth II visits Rhinsdale Residential Home on a visit to Scotland.

At the Christian heart of this United Kingdom stands Westminster Abbey, and it was right that it provided the setting for two events this year, one of them almost unbearably sad, and one, for Prince Philip and me, tremendously happy.

Joy and sadness are part of all our lives.

Indeed, the poet William Blake tells us that: "Joy and woe are woven fine, A clothing for the soul divine, Under every grief and pine runs a joy with silken twine".

This interweaving of joy and woe has been very much brought home to me and my family during the last months. We all felt the shock and sorrow of Diana's death.

Thousands upon thousands of you expressed your grief most poignantly in the wonderful flowers and messages left in tribute to her.

That was a great comfort to all those close to her.

But Prince Philip and I also knew the joy of our Golden Wedding. We were glad to be able to share this joy at Buckingham Palace with many other couples, who are celebrating their 50th anniversary this year.

Then, on our anniversary day, came a very different service at Westminster Abbey, this time "the silken twice", a service of thanksgiving for our 50 happy years together.

And, after that service, a chance to meet and chat to so many people.

I will never forget that day, nor a day five years ago when Windsor Castle suffered a terrible fire.

More than 100 rooms were badly damaged. They have now been fully renovated and they now look wonderful.

So the disaster of 1992 actually brought opportunities for all sorts of people to display their range of craftsmanship and skills, their love of history, and their faith in the future. Last month the restoration of the castle was completed and everyone involved gathered together to celebrate.

The castle is shortly to be open again for all to see – a mixture of the original with later additions and alterations – a vigorous blend of the old and the new.

And so it has been in the Commonwealth. Prince Philip and I were touched by the way the Canadian people welcomed us again to Canada.

We were delighted to be invited to visit Pakistan and India on the 50th anniversary of their Independence, and to celebrate their achievements since 1947.

The Prince of Wales represented Britain when the people of Hong Kong marked their return to China – in spectacular fashion.

Many of you might have felt a twinge of sadness as we in Britain bade them farewell.

The pictures speak for themselves, but we should be proud of the success of our partnership in Hong Kong and in how peacefully the old Empire has been laid to rest.

Out of the old Empire sprang the Commonwealth family of nations that we know today, and that, too, has grown and changed over the years.

In October, 51 representatives of Commonwealth governments met in Edinburgh, very much in the spirit of a family gathering. We all enjoy meeting old friends and making new ones, but there was also important business to be done.

For instance with the Prime Minister of Grenada, we discussed the drugs problem.

The world saw that the Commonwealth can make a major contribution to international relations and prosperity.

The meeting also showed that unity and diversity can go hand in hand.

Recent developments at home, which have allowed Scotland and Wales greater say in the way they are governed, should be seen in that light and as proof that the Kingdom can still enjoy all the benefits of remaining united.

Being united – that is, feeling a unity of purpose – is the glue that bonds together the members of a family, a country, a Commonwealth.

Without it, the parts are only fragments of a whole; with it we can be much more than the sum of those fragments.

For most of us this is a happy family day. But I am well aware that there are many of you who are alone, or bereaved, or suffering.

My heart goes out to you, and I pray that we, the more fortunate ones, can unite to lend a helping hand wherever it is needed, and not "pass by on the other side".

Saint Paul spoke of the first Christmas as the kindness of God dawning upon the world.

The world needs that kindness now more than ever – the kindness and consideration for others that disarms malice and which allows us to get on with one another with respect and affection.

Christmas reaffirms that God is with us today. But, as I have discovered afresh for myself this year, he is always present in the kindness shown by our neighbours and in the love of our friends and family. God bless you all and Happy Christmas.

1997

World Events of 1997
* Dolly the sheep is the first clone of an adult animal.
* Chinese leader Deng Xiaoping dies.
* The Labour party wins a landslide victory and Tony Blair becomes Prime Minister.
* A compensation fund for holocaust victims is set up in Switzerland.
* US space shuttle 'Atlantis' docks with the Russian 'Mir' space station.
* Diana, Princess of Wales, dies in a car crash in Paris.
* Forest fires in Indonesia cause widespread devastation.
* New Chinese President Tiang visits the USA.
* Hong Kong returns to Chinese rule.
* Over 125 countries sign a treaty banning landmines.
* Mother Teresa of Calcutta dies.

Sporting Life
* Golfer Tiger Woods, 21, becomes the youngest ever winner of the US Masters.
* The Grand National, postponed by a bomb scare, is won by 'Lord Gyllene'.

The Arts
* 'Titanic' wins the Oscar for best picture
* Arundhati Roy's 'The God of Small Things' wins the 29th Booker Prize
* 'A Taste of Cherry' by Iranian director Abbas Kiarostami won the Cannes Film Festival's Palme d'Or.
* Elton John's re-write of 'Candle in the Wind' in honour of Princess Diana sells over 35 million copies, with profits going to her charities.

Above:
The film 'Titanic' was launched in December and quickly established itself as one of the greatest blockbusters in cinema history.

Far left:
Reporter Andy Lyons presents flowers to Mother Teresa in the Bronx, New York

Left:
A Bouquet of flowers at Princess Diana's Funeral of the 6th September 1997 with a photograph of Diana the Princess of Wales.

1998

Above:
US President Bill Clinton, who was instrumental in bringing the conflicting parties together, meets the people of Northern Ireland with Tony Blair. Terrorists have been released as part of the agreement, but the IRA have so far not agreed to disarm.

Left:
Mourners queue up outside Beragh Roman Catholic Church twenty-four hours after Avril Monaghan and her baby daughter Maura were laid to rest in a shared grave. The Real IRA Car Bomb incident in Omagh, Northern Ireland in August 1998 was one of the worst atrocities in 30 years of troubles.

World Events of 1998
* President Clinton refuses to resign over the Monica Lewinsky scandal.
* A multi-party peace agreement is signed in Northern Ireland
* Economic recession hits Japan.
* The Real IRA who oppose the Good Friday agreement plant a bomb in Omagh, committing the worst atrocity in 30 years of troubles.
* Pol Pot, Cambodian leader responsible for the "Killing Fields" dies.
* India and Pakistan conduct nuclear tests.
* Water is discovered on the moon.

* Spain requests the extradition of ex-Chilean dictator General Pinochet, in hospital in London.
* US astronaut John Glenn, 77, who orbited the earth in 1962, goes into space to assist research into ageing.
* Scientists will not be allowed to clone humans.

Sporting Life
* France beat Brazil to win the World Cup.
* The International Amateur Athletic Federation names Ethiopian, Haile Gebrselassie, athlete of the year.

* Drug scandals overshadow the Tour de France. It is won by Marco Pantani – the first Italian to win for 33 years.

The Arts
* Steven Spielberg's 'Saving Private Ryan' is one of the year's best films,
* Shortly before his death, Ted Hughes publishes 'Birthday Letters', poems about his marriage to the ill-fated Sylvia Plath.
* The Portuguese writer José Saramago wins the Nobel Prize for Literature.

Christmas is a time for reflection and renewal. For Christians the year's end has a special and familiar significance, but all faiths have their calendars, their signposts, which ask us to pause from time to time and think further than the hectic daily round. We do that as individuals, with our families, and as members of our local communities.

It is not always easy for those in their teens or twenties to believe that someone of my age – of the older generation – might have something useful to say to them. But I would say that my mother has much to say to me. Indeed, her vigour and enjoyment of life is a great example of how to close the so-called generation gap. She has an extraordinary capacity to bring happiness into other people's lives. And her own vitality and warmth is returned to her by those whom she meets. But there are many of my mother's generation still with us. They can remember the First World War. Prince Philip and I can recall only the Second. I know that those memories of ours define us as old, but they are shared with millions of others, in Britain and the Commonwealth, people who often feel forgotten by the march of time. They remember struggles unknown to young people today, and which they will not forget. Nor should their countries forget them. And in recent days we have had another reminder of the courage and dedication shown so often round the world by our armed forces in the cause of peace.

Memories such as these are a consequence of age, and not a virtue in themselves. But with age does come experience, and that can be a virtue if it is sensibly used. Though we each lead different lives, the experience of growing older, and the joys and emotions which it brings, are familiar to us all. It is hard to believe that a half century has passed since our son, Charles, was christened, and now, last month, he has celebrated his 50th birthday. It was a moment of great happiness and pride on our part in all he has achieved during the last three decades.

As a daughter, a mother and a grandmother, I often find myself seeking advice, or being asked for it, in all three capacities. No age group has a monopoly of wisdom, and indeed I think the young can sometimes be wiser than us. But the older I get, the more conscious I become of the difficulties young people have to face as they learn to live in the modern world. We parents and grandparents must learn to trust our children and grandchildren as they seize their opportunities, but we can, at the same time, caution and comfort if things go wrong, or guide and explain if we are needed. My own grandchildren and their generation have a remarkable grasp of modern technology. They are lucky to have the freedom to travel and learn about foreign cultures at an age when the appetite for learning is keen. I see them pushing out the boundaries of science, sport and music, of drama and discovery.

Last June Prince Philip and I gave a party for 900 of Britain's Young Achievers. Buckingham Palace was brimming with young people who, in their short lives, have already set an example to us all. They are living proof that the timeless virtues of honesty, integrity, initiative and compassion are just as important as they have ever been. We hear much of "public life" – the hurly-burly of Parliament, the media, big business, city life. But for most people their contribution, at whatever age, is made quietly through their local communities just like so many of those Young Achievers. To most of them, service is its own reward. Their "public life" is their church, their school, their sports club, their local council.

My work, and the work of my family, takes us every week into that quiet sort of "public life", where millions of people give their time, unpaid and usually unsung, to the community, and indeed to those most at risk of exclusion from it. We see these volunteers at work in the organisations such as the Scouts and Guides, the Cadet Force, the Red Cross and St John's, the Duke of Edinburgh's Award Scheme and the Prince's Trust.

These organisations, and those who serve them so selflessly, provide the bridges across which the generations travel, meet and learn from one another.

They give us, with our families, our sense of belonging. It is they that help define our sense of duty. It is they that can make us strong as individuals, and keep the nation's heartbeat strong and steady too. Christmas is a good time for us to recognise all that they do for us and to say a heart-felt thank you to each and every one of them.

Happy Christmas to you all.

Left:
Queen Elizabeth II and Prince Philip arrive at Royal Ascot.

A very Happy Christmas to you from St George's Chapel, Windsor. Listening to the choir reminds me that this season of carols and Christmas trees is a time to take stock; a time to reflect on the events of the past year and to make resolutions for the new year ahead.

This December we are looking back not just one year, but on a hundred years and a thousand years. History is measured in centuries. More than ever we are aware of being a tiny part of the infinite sweep of time when we move from one century and one millennium to another.

Here at Windsor the first fortifications were started by William the Conqueror in the earliest years of this millennium. The castle we see today is the result of continual evolution and change over the last thousand years.

And as I look to the future I have no doubt at all that the one certainty is change – and the pace of that change will only seem to increase. This is true for all of us, young and old.

At my mother's 99th birthday last August I was struck how the inevitability of change affects us all, and how different were my mother's early years compared with those of my grandchildren.

Birthdays, like Christmas, are a good time to get the family together, and last summer we had all the generations well represented. My mother's birthday was also an opportunity to have a photograph taken of the four generations together.

As a family we cover quite a time-span. My mother can tell us about elderly relatives from her childhood whose memories went back into the middle of the 19th century. My grandchildren's experiences will in turn take them towards the end of the 21st century. For many of their generation the future is a source of excitement, hope and challenge.

Tonight I am giving a reception in Edinburgh for people under the age of 30 for all over Scotland. They have been invited because they have already achieved success or recognition in their lives. I am looking forward to hearing what they think about the future.

It is so encouraging talking to these young people. They are able to look forward to a future of opportunity and greater achievement. For others however the future is a cause of understandable anxiety.

There are many, for example of my generation, or amongst the more vulnerable in society, who worry that they will be left behind. The sheer rate of change seems to be sweeping away so much that is familiar and comforting. But I don't think we should be over-anxious. We can make sense of the future if we understand the lessons of the past. Winston Churchill, my first Prime Minister, said that "the further backward you look the further forward you can see". And it was this importance of history which was much in my mind when I opened the new Scottish Parliament in July this year.

Devolution in Scotland and Wales, and more recently the very welcome progress in Northern Ireland, are responses to today's changed circumstances, but they need to be seen in their historical contexts.

The Scottish Parliament is new, but its many links with the past were expressed through symbols and ceremony. Traditions are important all over the world. Last month on my visit to South Africa I went to a township school in Alexandra, outside Johannesburg, which has received financial aid from Britain.

Africa has a unique place in my affections; and there is always something so very special about the warmth and enthusiasm of the traditional African welcome. There was the same exuberance and happiness as I and other Commonwealth leaders arrived in Durban for the Commonwealth Heads of Government meeting.

Many of us at this conference highlighted how the varied strands of our shared history have been woven together so that we can more effectively address the challenges and opportunities ahead. Our common past has played a crucial part in bringing so many peoples together into the modern Commonwealth.

Looking out over the streets of Durban you quickly get a sense of how people from different cultures have come together. And it's the energy and creativity of this which is so very exciting. That to me is what the Commonwealth is all about. As with the process of devolution in the United Kingdom, the Commonwealth reminds us all of the importance of bringing the lessons of the past to bear on the aspirations for a better future.

Talking to Prime Ministers and Presidents in Durban, the need was brought home to me for all of us to draw from our history those constant and unchanging values which have stood the test of time and experience. Fairness and compassion, justice and tolerance; these are the landmarks from the past which can guide us through the years ahead.

These timeless values tell us above all about the way we should relate to people rather than to things. Thinking of others, not just of ourselves.

Earlier this year in Manchester I visited some of the emergency services, whose responsibilities day in and day out are based on concern for others. As always they are on duty over the Christmas and new year holidays. Some of these firefighters had gone well beyond Manchester to give assistance to others. Earlier this year this group had been working in very different conditions amongst the refugees in the Balkans.

Up and down the country people like these are working tirelessly to help others. They remind us of the responsibility of each and every one of us to show concern for our neighbours and those less fortunate than ourselves. I believe that this provides us with the direction and resolve required for the years ahead.

The future is not only about new gadgets, modern technology or the latest fashion, important as they may be.

At the centre of all our lives – today and tomorrow – must be the message of caring for others, the message at the heart of Christianity and all the great religions. This message – "Love thy neighbour as thyself" – may be for Christians 2000 years old. But it is as relevant today as it ever was.

I believe it gives us the guidance and the reassurance we need as we step over the threshold into the 21st century. And I for one am looking forward to this new millennium. May I wish you all a merry Christmas and, in this year of all years, a very happy new year.

1999

World Events of 1999

* The race is on to make the world's computer systems Y2K compliant before the end of the year.
* President Clinton survives the attempt to impeach him over the Monica Lewinsky scandal.
* A violent wave of attacks against Christians occurs in Pakistan.
* The health of President Yeltsin and Russian finances are a major cause for concern.
* King Hussein of Jordan dies.
* NATO launches an air attack on Serbia in an attempt to resolve the crisis in Kosovo.
* The Serbian leader, Slobodan Milosevic, could face trial for war crimes in Kosovo.
* Kurdish rebel leader Abdullah Ocalan is arrested by Turkish security forces in Nairobi and later sentenced to death.
* Genetically modified crops are at the root of the latest food scare.
* The murder of popular British TV presenter, Jill Dando, baffles police and shocks the nation.
* Nuclear powers India and Pakistan confront one another over Kashmir.
* Bertrand Piccard and Brian Jones complete the first non-stop circumnavigation of the globe in a hot air balloon.

Sporting Life

* In American basketball, Michael Jordan of the Chicago Bulls retires.
* The use of performance enhancing drugs is found to be widespread in all sports.
* Manchester United win the English Premier League, the FA Cup and the European Champion's League Cup.

The Arts

* Artefacts from Egyptian Pharaoh's tombs go on show in Paris.
* 'The Phantom Menace', a new 'Star Wars' movie starring Ewan MacGregor is released.
* Russia marks the 200th anniversary of the birth of the poet, Pushkin.
* Salman Rushdie's novel, 'The Ground Beneath Her Feet', wins the Booker prize.

Above:
A British pilot gets in to his Harrier Jet before he flew out of Gioia Del Colle Air Base in Italy, on a bombing raid of Yugoslavia

Left:
Liberated Kosovan Albanian refugees welcome NATO troops. However, there is doubt as to whether the issues facing the Balkan states can ever be resolved.

2000

Top Right:
Queen Mother's 100th Birthday Celebrations on Buckingham Palace Balcony looking out at crowds of well wishers.
Queen Mother, Prince Edward Earl of Wessex, Queen Elizabeth II, Prince Philip, Sophie Rhys Jones Countess of Wessex, Prince William.

Below:
Concorde taking off at Paris.

Far right:
Two of Britain's best loved and finest actors (top), Sir John Gielgud (1904-2000) and (below), Sir Alec Guinness (1914-2000) sadly died.

* Boxer Mike Tyson wins controversial come-back bout against Julius Francis in Manchester.
* Football legend Sir Stanley Matthews dies, aged 85.

The Arts
* The Tate Modern gallery on London's South Bank opens.
* The National Gallery commemorates the millennium with 'Seeing Salvation', based on the life of Christ.
* Margaret Attwood's 'The Blind Assassin' wins the Booker Prize.
* Actors Sean Connery and Michael Caine receive kinghthoods.
* Actors Sir John Gielgud and Sir Alec Guinness both die.
* The fourth volume of J.K. Rowling's Harry Potter books is published.

World Events of 2000
* The Serbian government collapses and Slobodan Milosevic forced to leave power.
* George W Bush is elected US President.
* Russian nuclear submarine 'Kursk' sinks, killing all on board.
* Air France Concorde crashes on take-off killing 113 people.

* 10,000 protestors descend on the IMF/World bank summit in Prague.
* Stonehenge opens to the public for the summer solstice for the first time since 1984.
* Floods in Mozambique kill thousands.
* Worst floods in England for 400 years.
* Siamese twins from Malta are separated against parents' wishes.
* The Queen Mother celebrates her 100th birthday.

Sporting Life
* Britain's best Olympic medal tally since 1920: 11 gold, 10 silver and seven bronze.
* Rower Steve Redgrave wins a record fifth consecutive Olympic gold medal.
* The Swede, Sven Goran Eriksson appointed manager of England's football team.
* England beats Ireland by a record 50 – 18 in the Six Nations (rugby) Tournament.

By any measure this Millennium year has been an unforgettable one. Since the turn of the year it has been celebrated and marked in this country and throughout the Commonwealth, and it has been a particular pleasure for me to visit Millennium projects large and small which will be reminders for generations to come of the time when the 21st century began.

But as this year draws to a close I would like to reflect more directly and more personally on what lies behind all the celebrations of these past 12 months.

Christmas is the traditional, if not the actual, birthday of a man who was destined to change the course of our history. And today we are celebrating the fact that Jesus Christ was born 2000 years ago; this the true Millennium anniversary.

The simple facts of Jesus' life give us little clue as to the influence he was to have on the world. As a boy he learnt his father's trade as a carpenter. He then became a preacher, recruiting 12 supporters to help him. But his ministry only lasted a few years and he himself never wrote anything down. In his early thirties he was arrested, tortured and crucified with two criminals.

His death might have been the end of the story, but then came the resurrection and with it the foundation of the Christian faith.

Even in our very material age the impact of Christ's life is all around us. The image of the Madonna and Child is particularly familiar to us during this Christmas season. If you want to see an expression of Christian faith you only have to look at our awe-inspiring cathedrals and abbeys, listen to their music, or look at their stained glass windows, their books and their pictures.

But the true measure of Christ's influence is not only in the lives of the saints but also in the good works quietly done by millions of men and women day in and day out through the centuries.

Many will have been inspired by Jesus' simple but powerful teaching: love God and love thy neighbour as thyself – in other words, treat others as you would like them to treat you. His great emphasis was to give spirituality a practical purpose.

Whether we believe in God or not, I think most of us have a sense of the spiritual, that recognition of a deeper meaning and purpose in our lives, and I believe that this sense flourishes despite the pressures of our world.

This spirituality can be seen in the teachings of other great faiths. Of course religion can be divisive, but the Bible, the Koran and the sacred texts of the Jews and Hindus, Buddhists and Sikhs, are all sources of divine inspiration and practical guidance passed down through the generations.

To many of us our beliefs are of fundamental importance. For me the teachings of Christ and my own personal accountability before God provide a framework in which I try to lead my life. I, like so many of you, have drawn great comfort in difficult times from Christ's words and example.

I believe that the Christian message, in the words of a familiar blessing, remains profoundly important to us all: "Go forth into the world in peace, be of good courage, hold fast that which is good, render to no man evil for evil, strengthen the fainthearted, support the weak, help the afflicted, honour all men."

It is a simple message of compassion and yet as powerful as ever today, 2000 years after Christ's birth.

I hope this day will be as special for you as it is for me. May I wish you all a very Happy Christmas.

Top:
Queen Elizabeth II with Pope John Paul II at the Vatican, October 2000.

Left:
Queen Elizabeth II with President Bill Clinton here pictured with his wife and daughter, Hilary and Chelsea Clinton at Buckingham Palace. The Clintons were on their last presidential visit to the UK.

Right:
Queen Elizabeth II and Prince Philip make a brief appearance on the balcony at the Trooping of the Colour, June 2001. The fly-past was cancelled when the heavens opened and everyone was soaked during this year's ceremony.

For many people all over the world, the year 2001 seems to have brought them more than their fair share of trials and disasters. There have been storms and droughts as well as epidemics and famine.

And this country has not been spared, with floods this time last year and foot-and-mouth, which has had such devastating consequences for our farmers and rural communities. They and others whose livelihoods have been affected continue to suffer hardship and anxiety long after newspaper headlines have moved on.

But whilst many of these events were of natural origin, it was the human conflicts and the wanton acts of crime and terror against fellow human beings which have so appalled us all. The terrorist outrages in the United States last September brought home to us the pain and grief of ordinary people the world over who find themselves innocently caught up in such evil.

During the following days we struggled to find ways of expressing our horror at what had happened. As so often in our lives at times of tragedy – just as on occasions of celebration and thanksgiving – we look to the Church to bring us together as a nation or as a community in commemoration and tribute.

It is to the Church that we turn to give meaning to these moments of intense human experience through prayer, symbol and ceremony.

In these circumstances so many of us, whatever our religion, need our faith more than ever to sustain and guide us. Every one of us needs to believe in the value of all that is good and honest; we need to let this belief drive and influence our actions. All the major faiths tell us to give support and hope to others in distress.

We, in this country, have tried to bring comfort to all those who were bereaved, or who suffered loss or injury in September's tragic events through those moving services at St Paul's and more recently at Westminster Abbey.

On these occasions and during the countless other acts of worship during the past year, we came together as a community – of relations, friends and neighbours – to draw strength in troubled times from those around us.

I believe that strong and open communities matter both in good times as well as bad. Certainly they provide a way of helping one another.

I would like to pay tribute to so many of you who work selflessly for others in your neighbourhood needing care and support.

Communities also give us an important sense of belonging, which is a compelling need in all of us. We all enjoy moments of great happiness and suffer times of profound sadness; the happiness is heightened, the sadness softened when it is shared.

But there is more than that. A sense of belonging to a group, which has in common the same desire for a fair and orderly society, helps to overcome differences and misunderstandings by reducing prejudice, ignorance and fear.

We all have something to learn from one another, whatever our faith – be it Christian or Jewish, Muslim, Buddhist, Hindu, or Sikh – whatever our background, whether we be young or old, from town or countryside.

This is an important lesson for us all during this festive season. For Christmas marks a moment to pause, to reflect and believe in the possibilities of rebirth and renewal.

Christ's birth in Bethlehem so long ago remains a powerful symbol of hope for a better future. After all the tribulations of this year, this is surely more relevant than ever.

As we come together amongst family and friends and look forward to the coming year, I hope that in the months to come we shall be able to find ways of strengthening our own communities as a sure support and comfort to us all – whatever may lie ahead.

May I, in this my 50th Christmas message to you, once again wish every one of you a very happy Christmas.

2001

World Events of 2001

* Foot and mouth disease devastates British farming.
* Millions journey to Allahabad for a religious festival by the Ganges.
* Dennis Tito becomes the world's first space tourist, paying $14m for a ride on a Russian rocket.
* Lord Jeffrey Archer is jailed for four years for fraud.
* Two trains collide near Selby after a motor vehicle plunges onto the line.
* Almost 5,000 people feared dead after suicide attackers fly planes into New York's World Trade Centre.
* Anthrax is sent by unknown terrorists through the US post.
* Labour wins a general election with 167 majority.
* Iain Duncan Smith is elected leader of the Conservative Party in place of William Hague.

* Timothy McVeigh, the Oklahoma bomber, is executed.
* Doctor Harold Shipman is jailed for the murder of 15 patients.

Sporting Life

* England beat Germany 5 – 1 in Germany, in a World Cup qualifying match.
* Racing driver Michael Schumacher wins his fourth World Championship.
* David Beckham scores a 90th minute goal for England against Greece to ensure a place in the 2002 World Cup finals.
* Indian batsman Sachin Tendulker becomes first man to score 10,000 runs in one-day games.

* Goran Ivanisevic becomes the first "wild card" winner of Wimbledon.
* Liverpool win both the FA Cup (against Arsenal) and the UEFA Cup (against Alares).
* Jonathan Edwards wins the triple jump at the World Athletics Championship.
* Lennox Lewis becomes world heavy-weight champion for the third time.

The Arts

* R and B star singer Aalyah dies in a plane crash, aged 22.
* 'Harry Potter and the Philosopher's Stone' becomes biggest-grossing film.
* The first part of the film trilogy 'The Lord of the Rings' is released.
* Former Beatle George Harrison dies of cancer, aged 58.
* The pop band Manic Street Preachers become the first western artistes to play in Cuba in 20 years.
* Mary Whitehouse, campaigner for values in broadcasting, dies.
* Martin Creed wins the Turner Prize for lights that turn on and off.

Top left:
The devastating site of "Ground Zero", depicting the aftermath of the terrorist attack on the Twin Towers of the New York World Trade Centre on September 11th.

Centre:
Former Tory Deputy Chairman, Jeffrey Archer pictured with his wife after his successful libel action against the Daily Star newspaper in which he was awarded a total of £500.000 in damages. He was later charged and tried with perjury and perverting the course of justice and after being found guilty, was jailed for four years.

Left:
Goran Ivanisevic beats Pat Rafter in this years Wimbledon Tennis Championship finals and becomes the first ever "wild card" men's champion finalist.

We would like to thank Derek Williams for the introduction, Roger Judd for the design and layout,
and Robert Frederick Ltd for the 'news' pages and the photographs from *The 20th Century: A Reflection*.

We are grateful to the following Agencies for permission to reproduce the photographs as follows:

Hulton-Getty Photographic Library:
pages: 10; 13; 14; 17; 18; 21; 25; 26; 29; 30; 34; 37; 38; 41; 42; 45; 46; 49; 50; 53; 55; 56; 61; 62; 67.

Mirror Syndication International:
pages: 8; 20 centre; 23; 58 centre; 59; 60 right; 63 left; 64 bottom left; 65; 66 left and centre; 67; 68; 69 bottom; 70 left; 72; 74; 75 left; 76; 77; 78; 79; 81; 83 bottom left and right; 85; 86; 87; 88 top right and left; 89; 90 bottom right; 91; 92; 93 top right; 94 bottom left; 95; 96 bottom left; 97; 98 bottom left; 98 bottom left; 99; 100; 101 bottom left and right; 102 top left; 103; 105 right; 106; 107; 108; 109.

British Library Cataloguing in Publication Data. A catalogue record for this book is available from the British Library.

Published by: Fifty, Downwood, Bath BA2 6DT
Eagle Publishing Ltd, PO Box 530, Guildford, Surrey GU2 4FH.

Printed and bound in Spain by Bookprint, S.L., Barcelona

ISBN 0 86347 546 9 (boxed presentation edition)
ISBN 0 86347 543 4 (jacketed hardback)